How much must we sell?

Managers are perpetually making decisions about extra running expenses, material price increases, asset acquisitions, pricing and the like. At the same time they need to manage the business to ensure that shareholders' profit expectations are satisfied. At the end of the day, sales must pay for all additional costs and borrowings. There is no other option. This book is designed to help sales managers and financial managers solve these problems together.

RONNIE DAVIDSON

DEDICATION

This book is dedicated to all those wishing to make a better life for all by growing businesses and economies through the sound application of business intelligence and maturely managing people's values.

You will never know how far your decisions will spread or how they will impact people's lives, so just do your very best and let integrity always prevail over profit.

Why should you buy this book?

You're a smart person, you are doing well at what you are good at. Your bosses are impressed with your results, there are promotion opportunities. BUT! Your bosses need someone who understands how to make profits.

Picture yourself sitting with your boss discussing the business. Imagine how impressed they will be when they hear your input on the financial impact of sales and marketing decisions.

Heard in the war room after the fuel price increase

Manager: "Fuel costs are increasing by 15% and we need to cover this increase from sales."

You: "We will need to increase sales by an extra R270 887 to pay for this increase and maintain our 7.87% return on sales? Of course we will need to fund the extra R2 183 00 in working capital through improved efficiencies"

No laptop, no abacus (what's an abacus?), just your sheer genius at work.

The rest of the team are gob-smacked and you are visualising your new position and the changes you will make as the new manager.

This workbook is aimed to help you deepen your understanding of how business decisions impact sales and how those confusing numbers actually work.

No matter what type of business you are in....

No matter what your professional qualifications are....

No matter what experience you have....

...every business and operating department is judged on its financial results.

To be a really successful manager, it is absolutely vital to understand the numbers.

"How Much Must We Sell" is easy reading with many examples and detailed spreadsheets to guide you. Once you grasp the concept it is a simple step to develop your own spreadsheets.

We start with basic stuff like how many units to breakeven and then develop to how much must we sell to achieve shareholder objectives.

The aim of this book is to assist you to make the connection between these decisions and their direct effect on sales. You will be enabled to answer these critical questions quickly and accurately:

"How much must you sell to pay for this decision?"

"Can we get this extra business?"

"Do we have capacity to deliver this extra business?"

"What impact on working capital requirements?"

Most important is that you will quickly gain deep understanding of the operational numbers concerning sales, profit and working capital.

I hope that you will enjoy reading it and, more importantly, that you will be able to apply the content to help you make **better business decisions**.

Above all I hope that this small investment delivers huge returns for you personally and whichever business employs you benefits from the extra value you will now add.

Regards and good luck

Ronnie Davidson

IMM, CPIM, CSCP, CISCP, CISCM

Founder of Business Learning Systems

www.businesslearning.co.za

email: rkd@businesslearning.co.za

CONTENTS

ACKNOWLEDGMENTS

I acknowledge all those thought pioneers who went before me and upon whose discoveries I now add this little brick of wisdom to the great wall of business knowledge.

1 GETTING STARTED

As the answers to the problems are built around the income statement using excel spreadsheets, it is suggested that you build your own spreadsheet to experiment with the formulas and solutions discussed in the workbook as you go along. This will help you develop your own model for use in your company.

You may enter your own values and percentages in the unshaded cells.

The common size percentages (CS%) are automatically calculated as a percentage of the sale value.

		Amount	CS %
Sales revenue		R 1 000 000	100,0%
Cost of sales	70%	R 700 000	70,0%
Gross profit		R 300 000	30,0%
Commission	2,50%	R 25 000	2,5%
Contribution		R 275 000	27,5%
SG&A - fixed costs		R 150 000	15,0%
Operating profit		R 125 000	12,5%
Interest expense		R 285	0,0%
Other income		R 1 045	0,1%
Net before tax		R 125 760	12,6%
Tax	29%	R 36 470	3,6%
Net income		R 89 290	8,9%

NOTE: At the end of each section there are exercises for you to practice. The answers to these will be found at the back of the manual.

You may want to refresh your memory by reviewing the glossary of business terms used in this book on the following pages.

Enjoy,

Ronnie

2   GLOSSARY OF TERMS

Accounts payable

Accounts payable, also known as creditors, are those accounts to whom the company owes money. Accounts payable are part of current liabilities or debt, and are recorded on the balance sheet.

Accounts payable days

The relationship between the accounts payable balance and the current rate of sales at cost price. Accounts payable days are used to monitor the number of days' cost of sales still unpaid. If the accounts payable balance is R500 000 and the daily sales at cost price are R10 000 then, at the current rate of selling, we have 50 days' sales that have not yet been paid for. It forms part of the cash conversion cycle.

Accounts receivable

Also known as debtors. Accounts receivable are the records of customers that have purchased goods or services but still owe the company money. They are recorded on the balance sheet under current assets.

Accounts receivable days

The relationship between the accounts receivable balance and the current rate of sales at selling price value.

Accounts receivable days is used to track our rate of selling to monies still owing for unpaid sales. If the accounts receivable balance is R450 000 and the daily sales are R15 000 then, at the current rate of selling, we have 30 days' sales that have not yet been paid for. It forms part of the cash conversion cycle.

Assets

Anything that the company owns is an **asset**. These may be current assets or non-current assets.

Cash conversion cycle

The cash conversion cycle or cash cycle measures the time it takes from the outflow to pay our suppliers for inventory to the inflow when we receive payment from our customers. Long cash cycle days require more funding from the company. If the cash conversion cycle is negative then our customers will be financing our business to a much greater day.

Cash conversion days, or cash cycle days, are calculated as follows:

Accounts receivable days + inventory days – accounts payable days.

If we have accounts receivable days of 45, inventory days of 65 and accounts payable days of 50 then our cash cycle days will be 60 days. From the time we pay our suppliers we must wait 60 days to receive our cash from our customers

Common size ratio

This useful ratio expresses all line items (expenses and profits), on the income statement as a percentage of sales revenue. It is most useful for analysing changes in expenses and profits in relation to changes in sales revenue. By tracking the changes in common size ratios or percentages we can readily see how the company is performing over time as well as against other similar operations.

Creditors

See accounts payable.

Current assets

These are assets owned by the company that are most likely to be converted into cash in the next twelve months. They include cash, accounts receivable, inventories (raw materials, work in progress(wip) and finished goods), and other current assets such as deposits, loans, prepayments etc....

Current liabilities

These are amounts owed by the company that will be paid out in the current financial year and represent the potential cash outflows in the current year. Current liabilities include accounts payable, tax due, dividends due, prepayments and deposits received.

Depreciation

Essentially it is spreading the cost, or expense, of using a non-current asset over its projected income producing life. If the asset is purchased for R1 000 000 and will produce for 10 years then, we will typically spread the expense, or cost, over 10 years at R100 000 per year. The time scale and technique used will vary according to the asset and the industry type.

Dividends

Dividends is the amount of after tax profit paid out to ordinary shareholders for the use of the share capital invested in the business. The amount paid is not fixed and will vary in line with the performance of the company, its cash position and the need to retain profits for investing in expansion.

Earnings

The term is interchangeable with profit and income. Earnings per share is the same as net profit per share. Earnings before interest and tax (EBIT) is the same as profit before interest and tax (PBIT)

Earnings per share

The net income attributable to the ordinary shareholders divided by the number of issued shares. The after tax profit per issued share.

Equity

Equity is also known as ordinary shareholders' interest. It is the ordinary share capital plus accumulated retained earnings and non-distributable reserves owing to the shareholders. It represents the owners' portion of the total investment in the business.

Expenditure

Not to be confused with expense. Expenditure is the actual payment for goods or services, and constitutes a cash outflow at the time it occurs. Expenditure can be for assets, expenses, and reducing liabilities.

Expense

May also be referred to as costs. Not to be confused with expenditure.

To "expense" something is to take it into account in the income statement in the same period the goods or services are used or consumed, irrespective of when the payment or expenditure takes place. Expenses reduce profit; expenditure reduces cash.

Fixed costs (period costs)

These costs (or expenses), may well vary from month to month but not as a direct result of fluctuations in sales. They are also referred to as operating expenses and SG&A (Selling, General and Administrative) expenses. Salaries, wages, rent, electricity, leases, depreciation, stationery, telephone, petrol and insurances are some examples of fixed costs.

Gross profit

The profit after cost of sales, have been deducted.

Sales – Cost of Sales = Gross profit

Inventory

Inventory is also referred to as stock. Inventory includes raw materials, work in progress and finished goods. It forms part of current assets in the balance sheet.

Inventory days

The number of days' inventory held in stock based on the current rate of sales at cost price. If the inventory balance is R600 000 and the daily sales at cost price are R10 000 then, at the current rate of selling, we have enough inventory to last 60 days.

Investment

The total funding to finance the business. It will comprise owners' equity plus interest-bearing debt such as loans and overdrafts plus non-interest bearing debt such as accounts payable.

Mark up

To mark up is to determine the selling price from the cost price. A mark up of 50% means that 50% of the cost price is added to the cost price to arrive at the selling price.

Net income (profit)

The profit after the tax has been deducted, but before dividends have been deducted. Also referred to as net profit after tax as well as attributable earnings.

Non-current assets

Those assets owned by the business for the long-term production of revenue. They are not expected to be converted into cash in the current financial year. Plant, IT equipment, property, buildings, patents, goodwill, R & D (Research and Development), and vehicles purchased are some examples of non-current assets. These are found under assets on the balance sheet.

Operating income

The profit after all fixed costs have been allowed for but before interest, other income and taxation. The actual trading profit from sales revenue after cost of sales and fixed costs are deducted. Also referred to as the EBIT (earnings before interest and tax), PBIT (profit before interest and tax), or controllable income.

Owners' equity

See equity.

Retained earnings

That portion of attributable income not paid to the ordinary shareholders in the form of dividends but retained, or reinvested, in the business as a source of funds. The retained earnings for the period will increase the accumulated retained earnings and are recorded as a liability under equity on the balance sheet.

Revenue (sales)

Income generated from invoiced sales at selling price excluding VAT or sale tax. Revenue increases profit irrespective of whether the sales have been paid or not. It appears on the income statement.

Share capital

The amount of money raised by issuing shares, or ownership, in the business. It is the capital raised from the company issuing shares and not related to the current trading price on the stock markets.

Variable costs

Any costs (expenses) directly incurred from selling the goods or services offered by the company. Cost of sales and sales commission will vary in line with the amount sold in the period. If there are no sales there will be no variable costs.

Working Capital

Also known as net current assets. Working capital is the difference between current assets and current liabilities. This is discussed in chapter 8.

3   COST BEHAVIOUR

As we will be examining the income statement in more detail to establish the relationship between costs, profit and the sales required to meet both, it is important for us to understand the various cost behaviours.

The formulas we will introduce are firmly based on a thorough understanding of which costs are truly variable and which are not.

There are essentially four different types of costs, that you will encounter in your business:

- variable costs
- fixed costs (selling, general and administration)
- semi-variable costs
- stepped costs

3.1   Variable costs

A variable cost is any cost that is directly proportional to sales. If there are no sales, there are no variable costs. Cost of sales is a good example of a variable cost.

Item on the income statement	Example A With sales	Example B No sales
Sales revenue	R 100 000,00	R -
Cost of goods sold (COS)	R 60 000,00	R -
Gross profit	**R 40 000,00**	**R -**
Sales commission	R 2 000,00	R -
Net Contribution from sales	**R 38 000,00**	**R -**
Fixed or period costs	R 12 000,00	R 12 000,00
Operating profit/(loss)	**R 26 000,00**	**-R 12 000,00**

When you buy inventory for resale you will record this as an asset owned by the company rather than a profit eating expense. Remember that it only becomes an expense or cost when the inventory is consumed. It lies in the warehouse as a current asset owned by the company and recorded as such on the balance sheet.

When the sale is made you will record the sale at selling price, and the value of the goods sold at cost price. Cost of goods sold, is now recorded as an expense against the sales made on the income statement. The inventory has been used or consumed in generating the sale.

The cost of sales is directly dependent on the sales in the period.

Sales commission is another example of a variable cost. If no sales are made in the period then the sales force will earn no sales commission. Commission is directly dependent on the sales revenue generated.

3.2 Fixed costs

We also refer to these as selling, general and administrative costs or "SG&A" costs, overheads or operating costs. They are the monthly costs of running the business irrespective of how much is sold.

These costs are also referred to as period costs as they are the costs incurred in each period.

These costs are not really "fixed" because they can change. Your telephone account will vary from month to month based on the number of calls you make but it will not vary directly in relationship to the sales you are making.

Salaries can vary from month to month depending on employee levels but are still regarded as being "fixed". If you sell nothing in the month, you will be hard-pressed explaining to your staff that they will not be paid.

Water and electricity are not the same every month, they too can vary, but not depending on sales volume. Of course some months are five weeks and others are only four weeks which also vary costs.

So a fixed cost or expense is one that may vary from period to period but is not directly linked to the changes in the sales volume or revenue.

3.3 Semi-variable costs

These costs, whilst not directly proportional to sales volume, are affected by changes to sales patterns and these cost patterns will be in line with the pattern of sales.

Distribution costs are an example of these semi variable costs. If sales are booming, the fleet is very busy with fully laden trucks rushing orders to the anxiously waiting customers.

You may be making 100 deliveries of five tons, or 500 tons of goods in the good months, but when sales decrease the number of deliveries may also decrease but not proportionate to the sales volume. The trucks will now be less full than previously. Instead of 100 deliveries of five tons per delivery, you are reduced to 80 deliveries of two tons each.

The number of tons dropped from 500 tons to 160 tons, is a 68% decline, whilst the number of deliveries dropped from 100 to 80, being a 20% decline. It may also be that the fixed cost element of leasing/depreciation and crew costs exceed the variable costs of fuel and running costs.

3.4   Stepped costs

These costs will support the particular level of activity until that cost resource is over-stretched. At this time extra costs are incurred to expand the resources and will remain static whilst sales continue to increase until they again need to be increased.

Customer support costs may throw further light on this element of cost. One support person may be handle up to 1 000 enquiries per month.

As soon as the enquiries reaches 1 010 this resource is over stretched and an extra resource is employed. Because of the combination of the two working together, these costs are able to handle 2 400 between them before a third resource is employed. These costs step up at a certain point of sales volume then remain fixed for a number of periods until the next step up in costs is required.

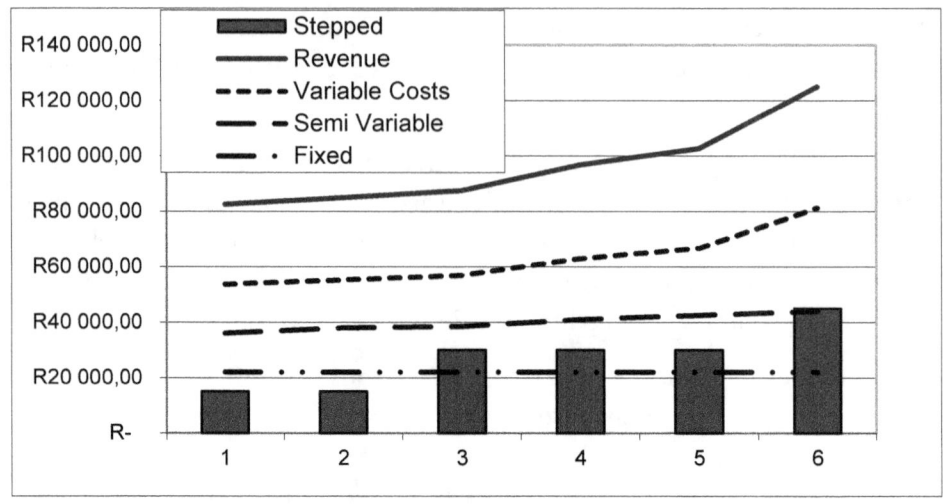

For our purposes we will regard costs as being either variable or not.

Exercise 1. Understanding cost behaviour

Simply identify each cost as being:

F: for fixed costs

V: for variable costs

S: for stepped costs

SV: for semi-variable

	F	V	S	SV
Wages				
Quality control				
Warehouse costs				
Cost of sales				
Outsourced transport				
Service desks				
Office space for growing sales force				
Depreciation				
Royalties on sales				
Consultants fees				

Notes for my business plan

4   PROFIT + COSTS = SALES

When setting the sales targets, the first criteria is to ensure that you at least recover your manufacturing or purchased costs, unless the strategy is to lose money whilst establishing market share. Fine if you have a lot of money to back the business whilst you attack the market.

The second criteria is to recover all those fixed or period costs.

The third issue is to also cover the profit required to keep the shareholders happy with your performance and for you to keep your job.

4.1   Recovering manufacturing costs

Your first priority is to ensure that all your product costs are covered by the selling price.

The value of the finished goods' costs will include all the costs associated with acquiring and manufacturing the product until it is received into the finished goods warehouse. These would include:

- materials purchase price

- shipping costs

- duties and taxes

- inbound transport costs

- manufacturing conversion costs

- rental/cost of space

- asset usage cost for plant and equipment (depreciation)

- labour costs

- management costs - production

- electricity costs used in manufacturing

- water used in manufacturing

- allocation of rates and taxes

These costs will be carried in inventory on the balance sheet whilst in the warehouse and will transfer to cost of sales in the income statement when sold.

Cash will reduce by the value of materials purchased, wages paid and other costs incurred at the time of manufacturing but profit will only reduce through cost of sales expense when the product is eventually sold at a later period.

 You might want to ask your accountants to explain this timing of profits more clearly if you are a bit confused by this.

So our first objective is to recover the costs of manufacturing.

4.2 Recovering fixed costs and operating profit

Selling, General and Administrative costs (fixed costs) reduce profit in the same month they occur (period costs), irrespective of what was sold. Your final sales revenue value needs to recover these period costs as well.

Finally, you would also like to make some profit in return for your efforts so the gross profit or contribution from sales must be sufficient to also cover the targeted profit amount, typically the operating profit.

Therefore, it follows that:

Fixed costs + profit = required gross profit or contribution. Remember that the gross profit or contribution has already accounted for the cost price of the items sold.

Operating profit	R 15 000,00	+
Fixed costs	R 23 000,00	+
Gross profit	R 38 000,00	=

You have decided that you require a minimum of R15 000 profit before tax each month and your fixed costs amount to R23 000 per month.

Working "backwards" from the profit amount, you can arrive at the minimum gross profit to cover fixed costs and operating profit.

The minimum gross profit from sales must be R38 000 per month.

If you decide to start a business, selling your services as a consultant, you will probably start by stating how much money you would need to make in a year to sustain your lifestyle. You would have no variable costs in this business.

4.2.1   Approach 1 – no variable costs

Annual earnings	R 180 000,00	+
Fixed costs	R 100 000,00	+
Sales target	R 280 000,00	=

Let us say that you needed to make R180 000 before tax. You calculate the fixed costs of running your business as being R100 000 per annum. If this is achievable then you have a viable business.

Because you have no cost of sales, well nothing significant anyway, if you sell R280 000 per annum and pay your fixed costs of R100 000 you will walk away with the R180 000 needed to enjoy life. Of course, we assume that all your clients have paid you!

So with no variable cost of sales involved, the sales target is the sum of the profit required by the owners, plus the monthly costs of running the business.

This is typically the case for service type industries such as accounting, consulting and training.

4.2.2   Approach 2 – with variable costs

You now consider starting another business that involves refilling printer cartridges. The cost of the materials to refill a cartridge is R65.00 and you believe that you can make a gross profit of R35.00 on each cartridge refilled.

The selling price of your refilled cartridge will therefore be:

Cost price	R	65,00	+
Added value (GP)	R	35,00	+
Selling price	R	100,00	=

Given the same requirements as the first business, your profit must be R180 000 and the fixed costs are estimated at R100 000. You can now calculate the required sales revenue.

You will note that the cost price is 65% of the selling price and the gross profit is 35% of the selling price. It follows that the total gross profit target value will also be 35% of the total sales revenue. By dividing the gross profit target by the gross profit percentage of sales we can work back to the sales target.

$$Sales\ revenue = \frac{R280\ 000}{35\%} = R800\ 000$$

R 280 000 ÷ 35% = R800 000 sales revenue per annum.

If you achieve your objectives then your income statement will reflect the following:

Revenue	R 800 000,00	100,00%
Cost of sales (COS)	R 520 000,00	65,00%
Gross profit	R 280 000,00	35,00%
Expenses (fixed costs)	R 100 000,00	12,50%
Operating profit	R 180 000,00	22,50%

So, once you have arrived at the gross profit required by adding the fixed expenses and profit requirements, you can divide the total gross profit by the gross profit percentage to arrive at the required sales revenue to cover:

- Materials cost

- Monthly fixed expenses

- Required profit.

Could you have arrived at the answer as elegantly by starting with your estimate of how much you must sell?

NOTE: Gross profit two, or contribution, whatever you call it, is the profit after all direct or variable costs have been deducted from sales revenue.

In this next scenario we also pay 2% commission on sales which is a variable cost.

Staying with our logic we will now divide the R280 000 required to cover fixed costs and profit by 33%.

Gross Profit of 35% - Commission of 2% = Contribution of 33%

$$Sales\ revenue = \frac{R280\ 000}{33\%} = R848\ 485$$

The income statement will now reflect the following:

Revenue	R 848 485,00	100,00%
Cost of sales (COS)	R 551 515,25	65,00%
Gross profit	R 296 969,75	35,00%
Sales commission 2%	R 16 969,70	2,00%
Contribution	R 280 000,05	33,00%
Expenses (fixed costs)	R 100 000,00	11,79%
Operating profit	R 180 000,05	21,21%

We now have the correct sales value to accommodate the cost of sales and the sales commission and, after deducting the fixed costs, we still attain our profit target of R180 000.

Good stuff.

Exercise 2. Calculating sales revenue

Scenario 1:

You are selling products with an average gross profit percentage of 28%. The owners of the business require an operating profit of R1 500 000 per annum and you need to cover **monthly** running expenses of R200 000.

How much must you sell in total value?

Scenario 2:

The average cost of sales for your products is 70%. The owners of the business require an operating profit of R1 500 000 per annum and you need to cover **monthly** running expenses of R200 000.

How much must you sell in total value?

Notes for my business plan

5 HOW MANY UNITS MUST WE SELL?

In these exercises we set out to determine the **number of units** we must sell to meet the requirements.

We have two scenarios, one for a single product which is quite straight forward but good for introducing the process, and a slightly more complicated one where multiple products are involved.

5.1 Single product

5.1.1 Breakeven

Breakeven analysis determines the volume of **sales units** needed to cover the SG & A or fixed expenses.

Contribution is revenue minus <u>all</u> variable costs and is the profit contributed from sales revenue after all direct or variable costs such as cost of sales and commission are recovered. The contribution from sales must cover all fixed expenses and profits that follow.

When starting a business the minimum target may be to break-even and the business will make zero profit.

For our exercise we have assumed the fixed costs to be R38 000 and therefore the contribution must also be R38 000 to breakeven. Again we have taken sales commission to be 2%. The contribution percentage is 38%.

Sales = R38 000 ÷ 38% = R100 000

Revenue	R 100 000,00
Cost of sales (COS)	R 60 000,00
Gross profit	R 40 000,00
Sales commission 2%	R 2 000,00
Contribution	R 38 000,00
Expenses (fixed costs)	R 38 000,00
Operating profit	R -

Contribution R38 000 – Expenses R38 000 = R00 or breakeven

So we have seen that to breakeven the contribution must equal the fixed or SG & A expenses.

If we know the contribution from each unit then the number of units required to breakeven will simply be:

Total SG & A expenses ÷ each units contribution

Our example shows unit contribution to be:

Unit selling price	R	27,50
Unit cost price	R	15,00
Unit gross profit	R	12,50
Unit commission 2%	R	0,55
Unit contribution	R	11,95

We can calculate the number of sales units required to break even by dividing the SG & A costs by the unit contribution. Remember that to breakeven SG & A costs will equal total contribution from all units.

R38 000.00 (SG & A expenses) ÷ R11.95 (unit contribution) = 3 180 units. The income statement will reflect the following, excluding units sold and the unit price and costs of course:

	Units	Cost item		Value		CS%
Revenue	3 180	R	27,50	R	87 450	100,00%
Cost of sales (COS)	3 180	R	15,00	R	47 700	54,55%
Gross profit		R	12,50	R	39 750	45,45%
Sales commission 2%		R	0,55	R	1 749	2,00%
Contribution		R	11,59	R	38 001	43,45%
Expenses (fixed costs)				R	38 000	43,45%
Operating profit	Rounding error			R	1	0,00%

Every unit sold above 3 180 (required to cover SG & A Expenses) adds R11.95 to the operating profit.

You would need to confirm that you have the capacity to generate these volumes and that you will be able to sell them in the competitive market.

5.1.2 How many units to make a profit?

The principle is the same as breaking even described above, but now we need to know how much to sell to cover the required profit as well. We add the operating profit to SG&A costs to establish the total contribution to cover both and then divide by the unit contribution as we did before.

Calculate Unit Contribution		
Unit selling price	R	48,00
Unit cost price	R	30,00
Unit commission 2%	R	0,96
Unit contribution	R	17,04

Calculate units to sell		
Operating profit	R	120 000,00
SG & A costs	R	500 000,00
Total contribution	R	620 000,00
Unit contribution	R	17,04
Required units		36 384,98

	Units sold	Cost item		
Revenue	36 385	R	48,00	1 746 480
Cost of sales (COS)	36 385	R	30,00	1 091 550
Gross profit	36 385	R	18,00	654 930
Sales commission 2%		R	0,96	34 930
Contribution		R	11,59	620 000
Expenses (fixed costs)				500 000
Operating profit				120 000

The practice exercises are on the next page.

Exercise 3. Determine unit sales to break even

Using the data in the table, calculate the minimum number of units
for the company to break even.

Company A : Break Even Analysis	
SG & A costs	250 000,00
Unit cost price	178,23
Average market selling price	256,52
Added value over market average	15%
Calculate the selling price	
Deduct the unit cost price	
Equals the unit gross profit	
Enter SG & A costs	
Divided by unit GP value	
Equals the number of units	

Exercise 4. Units to recover profit and costs

Using the data in the table, calculate the minimum number of units for the company to achieve the operating profit (OP) target. Remember to allow for the sales commission paid on each unit sold.

Company A : Units to Meet OP target	
SG & A costs	250 000,00
Operating profit target	120 000,00
Unit cost price	178,23
Average market selling price	256,52
Sales commission	2%
Added value over market average	15%
Calculate the selling price	
Deduct the unit cost price	
Deduct the sales commission	
Equals unit gross contribution	
Enter the SG & A costs	
Plus operating profit target	
Equals gross profit target	
Divided by unit contribution	
Equals the number of units	

5.2   Multiple products?

Very few companies only sell one product so we need a means of solving the problem of how much to sell for each product to achieve the total operating profit.

The initial steps are the same as for the single product:

Total operating profit + SG & A = total contribution

Contribution ÷ contribution percentage = total sales

To solve this business problem requires the use of a planning bill of materials structure to roll out the total contribution to each product family or individual product.

For our purposes we will use four product families. It is an easy extension to roll the product families to the individual products in each family.

This is the historical data we have for each of the four product families:

	Group A	Group B	Group C	Group D
Average GP%	25,0%	35,0%	15,0%	20,0%
Average commission %	0,0%	2,5%	2,0%	3,0%
Contribution % of sales	25,0%	32,5%	13,0%	17,0%
Portion of total contribution	18,0%	24,0%	30,0%	28,0%

Historically our figures show that:

Product group A has 18% share of total company contribution

Product group B has 24% share of total company contribution

Product group C has 30% share of total company contribution

Product group D has 28% share of total company contribution

Given a total company contribution requirement of R1 000 000 then we would expect:

Product group A to achieve R180 000 contribution

Product group B to achieve R240 000 contribution

Product group C to achieve R300 000 contribution and

Product group D to achieve R280 000 contribution

Hopefully that should add up to R1 000 000.

For our example we will use the following data for each product group:

	Group A	Group B	Group C	Group D
Average GP%	25,0%	35,0%	15,0%	20,0%
Average commission %	0,0%	2,5%	2,0%	3,0%
Contribution % of sales	25,0%	32,5%	13,0%	17,0%
Portion of total contribution	18,0%	24,0%	30,0%	28,0%
Company operating profit	R14 578 652			
Company SG & A costs	R35 678 544			
Company contribution	R50 257 196			

So the total company contribution must be at least R50 257 196 to cover the SG& A expenses and still make an operating profit of R14 578 652. The next step is to apportion this amongst the four product groups.

Product Group A is expected to contribute 18% x R50 257 196 which amounts to R9 046 295.

	Group A	Group B	Group C	Group D
Average GP%	25,0%	35,0%	15,0%	20,0%
Average commission %	0,0%	2,5%	2,0%	3,0%
Contribution % of sales	25,0%	32,5%	13,0%	17,0%
Portion of total contribution	18,0%	24,0%	30,0%	28,0%
Company operating profit	R14 578 652			
Company SG & A costs	R35 678 544			
Company contribution	R50 257 196,00			
	Group A	Group B	Group C	Group D
Portion of total contribution	18,0%	24,0%	30,0%	28,0%
Contribution amount	R 9 046 295	R 12 061 727	R 15 077 159	R 14 072 015

We then divide the product group contribution by the product group contribution percentages to arrive at each group's sales target.

	Group A	Group B	Group C	Group D
Company operating profit	R 14 578 652,00			
Company SG & A costs	R 35 678 544,00			
Company contribution	R 50 257 196,00			
	Group A	Group B	Group C	Group D
Portion of total contribution	18,0%	24,0%	30,0%	28,0%
Contribution amount	R 9 046 295	R 12 061 727	R 15 077 159	R 14 072 015
Divided by % contribution	25,0%	32,5%	13,0%	17,0%
Equals total sales of	R 36 185 181	R 37 113 006	R 115 978 145	R 82 776 558

For planning purposes the sales and operations plan would identify certain products within each group as being a representative sample of that group or they may be satisfied with the typical average price for that group.

	Group A	Group B	Group C	Group D
Average GP%	25,0%	35,0%	15,0%	20,0%
Average commission %	0,0%	2,5%	2,0%	3,0%
Contribution % of sales	25,0%	32,5%	13,0%	17,0%
Portion of total contribution	18,0%	24,0%	30,0%	28,0%

	Group A	Group B	Group C	Group D
Company operating profit	R 14 578 652			
Company SG & A costs	R35 678 544			
Company contribution	R50 257 196			
	Group A	Group B	Group C	Group D
Portion of total contribution	18,0%	24,0%	30,0%	28,0%
Contribution amount	R9 046 295	R12 061 727	R15 077 159	R14 072 015
Divided by % contribution	25,0%	32,5%	13,0%	17,0%
Equals total sales of	R 36 185 181	R 37 113 006	R 115 978 145	R 82 776 558
Average selling price	R165,74	R185,65	R203,50	R385,78
Total average units	218 325	199 908	569 917	214 569

We will extend our exercise to convert the sales revenues for each group to units by dividing the total sales by an average selling price.

Now that you have the model you can apply your own thinking to getting the best results for your own businessoperation.

The key idea here is this:

1. A known profit target supplied by management and added to planned SG & A costs based on history and adjusted for inflation, will arrive at a "known" contribution value.

2. Divide the known contribution value by a known contribution percentage and you have a very good chance of arriving at a realistic "known" revenue figure.

This model provides a first pass to see if you are in the ball park to meet the profit targets set by management and is used in those planning meetings to see how many sales units are required to meet the profit target.

If you start with sales revenues and work down to the operating profit it is kind of hit and miss. You discover that you are R1 000 000 short of the profit target so you need to make some changes. You reduce costs here, increase sales there and try again.

By the time you have balanced the books the plan on the spreadsheet may bear little resemblance to what will happen on the ground over the next twelve months and the reasons for the changes are lost in the murky depths of getting the spreadsheet to balance.

 We can always make a plan for capacity but if the market just will not bear those extra sales you need to rethink the strategy for that group.

Exercise 5. Determine unit sales for multiple groups

Using the data in the table below calculate how many units each product group needs to sell.

	Group A	Group B	Group C	Group D
Average GP%	27,0%	32,0%	18,0%	22,0%
Average commission %	2,0%	2,5%	2,0%	2,0%
Contribution % of sales				
Company operating profit	R12 000 000,00			
Company SG & A costs	R36 000 000,00			
Company contribution				
	Group A	Group B	Group C	Group D
Portion of total contribution	15,0%	12,0%	28,0%	45,0%
Contribution amount				
Divided by % contribution				
Equals total sales of				
Average selling price	R175,00	R210,00	R238,00	R410,00
Total average units				

Notes for my business plan

6   DEGREE OF OPERATING LEVERAGE (DOL)

Degree of Operating Leverage (DOL), links the operating profit directly to the sales revenue.

This is a most useful formula to quickly calculate the impact on operating profit for any change in revenue.

You could of course rerun your income statement spreadsheet to arrive at the same answer if you have your PC available or have access to the income statement at that point.

DOL solves the problem very simply and is a most useful tool in "What If" scenarios, particularly to turbo-charge your career in those competitive planning meetings.

6.1   Impact of change in sales

Let us take a closer look at this technique.

As you now understand the difference between variable and fixed costs (just in case you were sketchy before), you can now apply this knowledge in using DOL.

DOL is a factor that expresses the relationship between fixed and variable costs.

To see this in practice examine the table below:

	Company A		Company B	
Revenue	R	100 000,00	R	100 000,00
COS	R	70 000,00	R	5 000,00
Gross profit	R	30 000,00	R	95 000,00
SG & A expenses	R	16 500,00	R	81 500,00
Operating profit	R	13 500,00	R	13 500,00

You will note that whilst both companies have generated the same operating profit from the same revenue, Company A has higher variable costs than Company B and Company B has higher fixed costs than Company A. Company A is your typical manufacturing or trading company whilst Company B resembles a typical services organization such as auditing or advertising.

The DOL is calculated by dividing the gross profit by the operating profit.

 If there are other variable costs such as commission then you would divide the operating profit by the contribution amount after all variable costs.

DOL for Company A is: $\frac{30\ 000}{13\ 500} = 2.222$ the DOL factor

DOL for Company B is: $\frac{95\ 000}{13\ 500} = 7.037$ the DOL factor

Okay, so what now?

The sales for both companies are expected to increase by 12.5%. How will this affect the operating profit for both?

By multiplying the DOL factor by the percentage change in sales you will immediately determine the impact on the operating profit.

Company A's operating profit will increase by:

   (12.50% x 2.222) or 27.77% of R13 500 = R3 749.99

Operating profit for Company A will be

   R13 500.00 + R3 749.99 = R 17 249.99

Company B's operating profit will increase by

   (12.5% x 7.037) or 87.96% of R13 500 = R11 874.87

Operating profit for Company B will be

   R13 500.00 + R11 874.87 = R25 374.87

Time to put this to the test:

	Company A	Company B
Revenue	R 112 500,00	R 112 500,00
COS	R 78 750,00	R 5 625,00
Gross profit	R 33 750,00	R 106 875,00
SG & A expenses	R 16 500,00	R 81 500,00
Operating profit	R 17 250,00	R 25 375,00

Okay so we are out by a few cents here and there due to the number of decimals used in the DOL, but pretty good results wouldn't you say?

From the two examples you can see that companies with a high DOL will receive better improvement in operating profit for any increase in sales due to the low variable cost content and vice versa.

6.2   Impact of change in operating profit

Of course you can also use DOL to work backwards from the required percentage increase in operating profit to the effect on sales.

In order to increase shareholders' earnings, management requires an increase of 28% in operating profit (quite steep I'd say). How much more must we sell to meet this expectation?

For our example we will use the DOL for both companies, 2.22 and 7.04.

In order to increase Company A's operating profit by 28% how much must sales increase?

$$\frac{28.0\%}{2.22} = 12.6\% \text{ extra sales}$$

You recall that the first example was a 12.5% increase but, hey, you are not designing a fail-safe, fool-proof jet fighter. A few little decimal places and rounding will not prove catastrophic.

Company B would be $\dfrac{28.0\%}{7.04} = 3.98\%$ increase in sales.

You are not trying to change the DOL factor from 2 to 8 but just need to know what the factor is for your company at that point in time. It could of course progressively alter as fixed costs might increase more than variable costs due to changing business conditions.

The purpose of these useful formulas is to take the guesswork out of business and sales planning. They greatly assist us to answer the compelling question, "if something changes how much more must we sell?" with a quick and accurate answer to assess if the sales are achievable and capacity is available to cover the change without reducing profits and ultimately shareholders' wealth.

Exercise 6. DOL

Using the data in the first table, answer the questions in the table below it:

	Company A	Company B
Sales revenue	285 000	465 000
Cost of sales	185 250	176 700
Gross profit	99 750	288 300
Sales commission	5 700	16 275
Contribution	94 050	272 025
Bank charges	1 560	4 500
Advertising	12 000	56 000
Auditors fees	5 632	5 632
Rent	5 000	5 000
Salaries and wages	15 000	106 000
Insurance	22 236	22 236
Operating profit	32 622	72 657
Interest expense	5 600	4 231
NIBT	27 022	68 426

Question		A	B
1	Calculate the degree of operating leverage for the two companies.		
2	Which company would benefit more from an increase in sales?		
3	Sales increase by 12%. How much will each company's operating profit increase?		
4	If Company B wants to increase operating profit by 10%, how much more must they sell percentage wise?		

Notes for my business plan

7 MARGINS AND ADDED VALUE?

Every activity in business must be paid from sales.

By this stage, you have hopefully bought into the concept that working from profit back to sales is a more elegant method than starting with sales and seeing what profit you are left with.

Remember that revenue is second to profit and cash is always king.

This chapter develops the theme that any decision to increase expenses, buy assets, raise finance or increase EPS (earnings or profit per share) or ROE (return on equity) requires additional contribution from sales revenue to maintain the financial efficiency and wealth of the business.

It answers the question….

"If you do this, how much more must you sell to maintain the wealth of the business?"

Recap: You have so far seen that fixed or SG&A costs plus operating profit equals gross profit (or contribution) and that gross profit divided by gross profit margin (percentage) equals sales revenue.

	Company A	CS%	Company B	CS%
Operating profit	R 25 000 000		R 25 000 000	
SG & A expenses	R 69 000 000		R 69 000 000	
Gross profit	R 94 000 000	30%	R 94 000 000	20%
Sales revenue	R 313 333 333		R 470 000 000	

Gross profit margin is, as you know, the gross profit value expressed as a percentage of sales revenue. But, what is the gross profit margin actually a function of, in your business?

Gross Profit margin measures our ability to sell the added value that increases the profit and consequently the selling price.

Two companies are both trading in the same business environment with very similar products sourced from very similar suppliers. Company A boasts a gross profit margin of 26%, whilst Company B struggles along with margins of around 21%. What is the essential difference between the two companies?

Company A is able to sell their customers higher "added value".

Higher added value translates into higher margins. Higher margins require lower sales revenues and lower sales revenue needs less money tied up in working capital. (More about working capital later.)

Company B must sell 24% more than Company A to compensate for the 5% lower margin..

	Company A			Company B	
Operating profit	R	25 000 000		R	25 000 000	
SG & A expenses	R	100 000 000		R	100 000 000	
Gross profit	R	125 000 000	26%	R	125 000 000	21%
Sales revenue	R	480 769 231		R	595 238 095	24%

If they could find a way of increasing their margins from 21% to 26% they could reduce revenue by R114 468 864.47 or about 20%!

 TIP   *It is better to sell smarter than work harder.*

7.1   Margins and sales revenue

	Company A	Company B	Company C	Company D
Revenue	R 2 333 333	R 1 750 000	R 1 400 000	R 1 166 667
Gross profit margin	15%	20%	25%	30%
Gross profit	R 350 000	R 350 000	R 350 000	R 350 000
SG & A expenses	R 250 000	R 250 000	R 250 000	R 250 000
Operating profit	R 100 000	R 100 000	R 100 000	R 100 000

Examine the table above. Which company would you rather own: A, B, C, or D?

Most managers would opt for D even though its sales revenue is only 50% that of Company A!

Wow! What about this drive to sell more?

A good strategy is to increase margins through adding value that does not cost more. This could include, amongst others:

- Improved order fill rates

- Better on-time deliveries

- Lower order quantities delivered more frequently

- Lower scrap and rework costs

- Actively rotate stock to reduce write offs.Quicker flow through the plant

- Customer training

- Salesforce education on valued added selling

- Communicating the business value

- Efficient returns policies

- Where there is strategic business advantage to be gained by the customer talk to the strategic thinkers in the business.

 Added Value improves the customer's business process and must be worth paying your premium.

Exercise 7. Margins and sales revenue

1. The contribution from sales revenue must always be sufficient to cover the required operating profit plus SG & A expenses. Given this information and the contribution percentage, calculate the required sales revenue.

2. Once you have arrived at the revenue figure, prove your answer by completing the income statement below each answer under "proof".

3. Enter the sales revenue amount in the top cell of each option and by using the common size percentages complete the calculations for cost of sales, gross profit and sales commission and contribution.

Deduct the SG & A expenses and you should arrive at the calculated contribution which of course must equal the required contribution.

Once you have checked your answers we can move on to examine the mechanics and function of working capital as it also plays a role in determining the impact of extra sales on the business model.

		Scenario 1		Scenario 2		Scenario 3
Gross profit		30,00%		15,00%		25,00%
Commission		2,00%		0,00%		2,00%
Contribution		28,00%		15,00%		23,00%
SG & A expenses		400 000		400 000		400 000
Operating profit		250 000		250 000		250 000
	CS %	Proof	CS %	Proof	CS %	Proof
Sales revenue						
Cost of sales						
Gross profit						
Commission						
Calculated contribution						
Required contribution						
SG & A expenses						
Operating profit						

Notes for my business plan

8   UNDERSTANDING WORKING CAPITAL

We will now examine the management of working capital in more detail.

 You may want to run this past your accounting colleagues if you are not quite comfortable with this aspect of business.

8.1   Why it matters:

Taken from: http://www.investinganswers.com/financial-dictionary/financial-statement-analysis/working-capital-869

Working capital is a common measure of a company's liquidity, efficiency, and overall health. Because it includes cash, inventory, accounts receivable, accounts payable, the portion of debt due within one year, and other short-term accounts, a company's working capital reflects the results of a host of company activities, including inventory management, debt management, revenue collection, and payments to suppliers.

Positive working capital generally indicates that a company is able to pay off its short-term liabilities almost immediately. Negative working capital generally indicates a company is unable to do so. This is why analysts are sensitive to decreases in working capital; they suggest a company is becoming overleveraged, is struggling to maintain or grow sales, is paying bills too quickly, or is collecting receivables too slowly. Increases in working capital, on the other hand, suggest the opposite. There are several ways to evaluate a company's working capital further, including calculating the inventory-turnover ratio, the receivables ratio, days payable, the current ratio, and the quick ratio.

One of the most significant uses of working capital is inventory. The longer inventory sits on the shelf or in the warehouse, the longer the company's working capital is tied up.

When not managed carefully, businesses can grow themselves out of cash by needing more working capital to fulfill expansion plans than they can generate in their current state.

8.2 Defining working capital

Working capital is current assets minus current liabilities
If we sell all these assets for cash and settle the current debt what is over to run the business

In the table below we see a typical balance sheet scenario showing current assets and current liabilities. In our example the difference between the two results in working capital of R200 647.00

	Before
Cash	R 56 000,00
Accounts receivable	R 265 231,00
Inventory	R 192 445,00
Total current assets	**R 513 676,00**
Accounts payable	R 175 663,00
Short-term loans	R 52 366,00
Tax due to SARS	R 85 000,00
Total current liabilities	**R 313 029,00**
Working capital	**R 200 647,00**

Before moving on we need to clarify something right here and now.

Many delegates on my courses are exhorted to "reduce working capital" by their well-meaning managers but technically there is very little that operations people can do to reduce working capital.

Let us assume that some customers pay us an amount of R8 500.

	Before	Transaction	After
Cash	R56 000,00	R8 500,00	R64 500,00
Accounts receivable	R265 231,00	-R8 500,00	R256 731,00
Inventory	R192 445,00	R0,00	R192 445,00
Total current assets	*R513 676,00*	*R0,00*	*R513 676,00*
Accounts payable	R175 663,00	R0,00	R175 663,00
Short-term loans	R52 366,00	R0,00	R52 366,00
Tax due to SARS	R85 000,00	R0,00	R85 000,00
Total current liabilities	*R313 029,00*	*R0,00*	*R313 029,00*
Working capital	**R200 647,00**	**R0,00**	**R200 647,00**

Let's see what effect this transaction has on working capital.

The cash balance increases by the same amount as accounts receivable decreases, and, as both form part of current assets, current assets remain unchanged.

If current assets remain the same and the transaction has no effect on current liabilities, then it follows that working capital will also remain unchanged as a result of this transaction. So getting customers to pay has no effect on the level of working capital.

The same applies if we purchase inventory for cash.

We buy inventory valued at R12 500 for cash. See what happens to the current assets, current liabilities and working capital:

	Before	Transaction	After
Cash	R56 000,00	-R12 500,00	R43 500,00
Accounts receivable	R265 231,00	R0,00	R265 231,00
Inventory	R192 445,00	R12 500,00	R204 945,00
Total current assets	**R513 676,00**	**R0,00**	**R513 676,00**
Accounts payable	R175 663,00	R0,00	R175 663,00
Short-term loans	R52 366,00	R0,00	R52 366,00
Tax due to SARS	R85 000,00	R0,00	R85 000,00
Total current liabilities	**R313 029,00**	**R0,00**	**R313 029,00**
Working capital	**R200 647,00**	**R0,00**	**R200 647,00**

Because both transactions are within current assets, there is still no change to current assets. As the transaction does not impact current liabilities there is no change there either. If there is no change to either current asset or current liabilities then there will be no change to working capital either.

Okay, let us buy some inventory on terms from our suppliers (accounts payables). That should change the working capital.

Or will it?

As this transaction affects both current assets and current liabilities by the same amount of R12 500.00, [good bookkeeping], and both increase by the same amount, there is again no net change to working capital.

	Before	Transaction	After
Cash	R56 000,00	R0,00	R56 000,00
Accounts receivable	R265 231,00	R0,00	R265 231,00
Inventory	R192 445,00	R12 500,00	R204 945,00
Total current assets	*R513 676,00*	*R12 500,00*	*R526 176,00*
Accounts payable	R175 663,00	R12 500,00	R188 163,00
Short-term loans	R52 366,00	R0,00	R52 366,00
Tax due to SARS	R85 000,00	R0,00	R85 000,00
Total current liabilities	*R313 029,00*	*R12 500,00*	*R325 529,00*
Working capital	**R200 647,00**	**R0,00**	**R200 647,00**

One more try. We will pay accounts payable R18 500.00.

	Before	Transaction	After
Cash	R56 000,00	-R18 500,00	R37 500,00
Accounts receivable	R265 231,00	R0,00	R265 231,00
Inventory	R192 445,00	R0,00	R192 445,00
Total current assets	*R513 676,00*	*-R18 500,00*	*R495 176,00*
Accounts payable	R175 663,00	-R18 500,00	R157 163,00
Short-term loans	R52 366,00	R0,00	R52 366,00
Tax due to SARS	R85 000,00	R0,00	R85 000,00
Total current liabilities	*R313 029,00*	*-R18 500,00*	*R294 529,00*
Working capital	**R200 647,00**	**R0,00**	**R200 647,00**

There is still no change to working capital. How do we get this amount to change?

So far we have been dealing with transactions that affect the same time-period, the **current period**.

We will now expand our example to include the non-current time-period as well. We will issue R12 500 more in share capital

	Before	Transaction	After
Cash	R 56 000,00	R 12 500,00	R 68 500,00
Accounts receivable	R 265 231,00	R -	R 265 231,00
Inventory	R 192 445,00	R -	R 192 445,00
Total current assets	**R 513 676,00**	**R 12 500,00**	**R 526 176,00**
Accounts payable	R 175 663,00	R -	R 175 663,00
Short-term loans	R 52 366,00	R -	R 52 366,00
Tax due to SARS	R 85 000,00	R -	R 85 000,00
Total current liabilities	**R 313 029,00**	**R -**	**R 313 029,00**
Working capital	**R 200 647,00**	**R 12 500,00**	**R 213 147,00**
Non-Current Time Period			
Share Capital	R 100 000,00	R 12 500,00	R 112 500,00
Long-term loans	R 250 000,00	R -	R 250 000,00
Total non-current liabilities	**R 350 000,00**	R 12 500,00	**R 362 500,00**
Non-current assets	R 149 353,00	R -	R 149 353,00

At last, working capital has changed by the amount of the additional share capital sold.

Cash increased, current assets increased, but current liabilities remained unchanged. As a consequence working capital increased by R12 500.

What is the difference?

 The transaction has crossed the time line between current and non-current and so working capital changes.

So what can we learn from this exercise? We can improve cash but not increase working capital, in any of the following ways:

- Reducing inventories
- Collecting debtors
- Increasing accounts payable.

We can increase cash and working capital through:

- Finance from share capital

- Long-term loans

- Profitable cash sales

Getting back to your manager's exhortation for you to reduce working capital...

Considering what is really under your influence, it is highly unlikely that you could ever please him and he will just have to forfeit his bonus based on reducing working capital!

What he really means is that you need to generate cash. Most operations managers see working capital as only comprising accounts receivable, inventory and accounts payable.

At an operational level, our most important task is to generate the cash and the best way to do this is by:

- Controlling and collecting accounts receivable

- Keeping inventory levels at the lowest possible levels without disrupting service levels

- Extending payment to accounts payables without annoying suppliers

- Selling profitably for cash, or short payment terms

What does this have to do with sales revenue and the impact of making decisions that require extra sales?

Great question!

If sales increase and all else remains, the working capital will increase proportionately. If sales increase by 10%, then working capital will also increase by 10%. If working capital increases by 10%, then cash is consumed to finance the increased debtors and inventory levels.

8.3 How do we measure working capital?

The major items included under working capital are accounts receivable, inventory and accounts payable. We are excluding cash for this exercise.

In order to manage these amounts we must measure them against prevailing sales revenue [for accounts receivable] and cost of sales [for inventory and accounts payable]. The idea is simply to ensure that the relationship between the daily rate of selling and these three areas of working capital remain consistent or improve.

We will use the following table for our exercises:

Income Statement	Last Year	
	Annual	Daily
Sales revenue	R 365 000,00	R 1 000,00
Cost of sales	R 255 500,00	R 700,00
Balance sheet	Balance	Days
Accounts receivable	R 45 000,00	45
Inventory	R 42 000,00	60
Current assets	*R 87 000,00*	
Accounts payable	R 38 500,00	55
Current liabilities	*R 38 500,00*	

8.3.1   Accounts receivable days

This is calculated by dividing the accounts receivable balance by the current daily sales. It tells us how many days sales, at the current daily rate of selling, are not yet paid, and helps us to compare the time taken for customers to pay from one year to the next relative to the sales for that year.

In our table, the daily sales are R1 000.00 per day and the accounts receivable balance is R45 000.00.

The accounts receivable days are therefore R45 000.00 ÷ R1 000.00 = 45 days of current daily sales not paid.

8.3.2 Inventory days

Inventory days is the number of daily sales at cost price held in stock, or how long it takes to sell the inventory. We can compare the inventory days to previous years to see if the inventory is increasing, or decreasing, in relation to prevailing sales rates.

Because inventory is at cost price, we use daily cost of sales for the calculation.

Using our example, the inventory balance of R42 000.00 is divided by the daily cost of sales of R700.00 giving us 60 days of current sales in inventory. It will take 60 days to empty the warehouse.

8.3.3 Accounts payable days

This calculates how long we are taking to pay our suppliers based on the daily cost of sales to determine if we are extending or shortening our payment terms.

Accounts payable balance ÷ daily cost of sales.

Our example reflects the total due to suppliers (accounts payable) as being R38 500. Given that we are selling inventory at the rate of R700 per day it follows that:

R38 500 ÷ R700 = 55 days of inventory sales unpaid.

8.4   Increase in sales and impact on cash

If revenue increases by 10% and customers take the same time to pay, i.e. 45 days, then accounts receivable will increase by the same percentage as sales, being 10%. We would also need to purchase and carry more inventory to support the sales increase.

Time to test the concept with figures:

| Income Statement | Last Year | | This Year | | % Change |
	Annual	Daily	Annual	Daily	
Sales revenue	R 365 000	R 1 000	R 401 500	R 1 100	10,00%
Cost of sales	R 255 500	R 700	R 281 050	R 770	10,00%
Balance sheet	Balance	Days	Balance	Change	
Accounts receivable	R 45 000	45	R 49 500	R 4 500	10,00%
Inventory	R 42 000	60	R 46 200	R 4 200	10,00%
Current assets	**R 87 000**		**R 95 700**	**R 8 700**	**10,00%**
Accounts payable	R 38 500	55	R 42 350	R 3 850	10,00%
Current liabilities	**R 38 500**		**R 42 350**	**R 3 850**	**10,00%**

More debtors means less cash and more inventory to support service levels for increased sales means less cash.

So all the relevant balances have increased by the same ratio as the sales increase and working capital increases by R4 850.00 or 10%. The increased working capital will decrease cash by the same amount, R4 850.00.

The important message is that if these performance measurements remain the same as last year and sales increase, these balances will increase proportionately.

The good news is that the company is at least maintaining these efficiencies or performance ratios in line with last year.

 It is important to know this as many start-up businesses go bust because the rapid increase in sales cannot be funded by the increased cash required to fund the increased working capital.

If accounts receivable or inventory increased by more than 10%, then this would be reflected in an increase in the "days" for these balances and would show we are becoming less efficient in managing our working capital.

8.5 Monitoring working capital

8.5.1 Using days

We will use the data in the following table for our explanation.

Income Statement	Last Year		This Year		% Change
	Annual	Daily	Annual	Daily	
Sales revenue	R 365 000	R 1 000	R 401 500	R 1 100	10,00%
Cost of sales	R 255 500	R 700	R 281 050	R 770	10,00%
Balance sheet	Balance	Days	Balance	Days	
Accounts receivable	R 45 000	45	R 55 000	50	22,22%
Inventory	R 42 000	60	R 49 500	64	17,86%
Current assets	R 87 000		R 104 500	R 17 500	20,11%
Accounts payable	R 38 500	55	R 42 350	R 55	10,00%
Current liabilities	R 38 500		R 42 350	R 3 850	10,00%
Working capital	R 48 500		R 62 150	R 13 650	28,14%

In this example an increase of 10% in sales resulted in an increase of 28.14% in working capital due to customers taking longer to pay and carrying more inventory than we needed to service last year's sales.

It is now a quick exercise to compare last year's performance to this year by simply comparing the "days". Accounts receivable increased by 5 days from 45 to 50 reflecting an 11% drop in collection performance. Inventory went from carrying 60 days of sales to service customers to 64 days of inventory.

These inefficiencies incurred a negative cash flow of R13 650.00 as working capital increased to R62 150 from R48 500 or 28%. Ten percent of this increase is due to the increases in sales but 18% is due to increased inventory levels and later payments. Not so good!

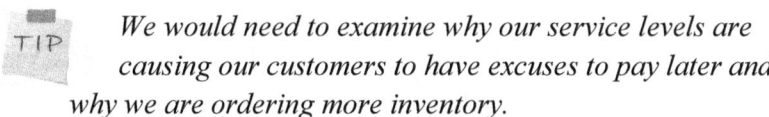 *We would need to examine why our service levels are causing our customers to have excuses to pay later and why we are ordering more inventory.*

In a nutshell:

- if the performance "days" remain then any increase in sales will increase working capital by the same percentage

- any increase in working capital requires extra cash to finance the increase

As a strategy to fund growth internally you could of course tighten controls to increase efficient management of working capital reduce the debtors and inventory days to offset the cash required to grow.

The following table shows that whilst sales increased by 10% there was no change to working capital.

Income Statement	Last Year		This Year		% Change
	Annual	Daily	Annual	Daily	
Sales revenue	R 365 000	R 1 000	R 401 500	R 1 100	10,00%
Cost of sales	R 255 500	R 700	R 281 050	R 770	10,00%
Balance sheet	Balance	Days	Balance	Days	
Accounts receivable	R 45 000	45	R 47 350	43	5,22%
Inventory	R 42 000	60	R 43 500	56	3,57%
Current assets	R 87 000		R 90 850	R 3 850	4,43%
Accounts payable	R 38 500	55	R 42 350	R 55	10,00%
Current liabilities	R 38 500		R 42 350	R 3 850	10,00%
Working capital	R 48 500		R 48 500	R -	0,00%

The company reduced the time waiting for customers to pay from 45 days to 43 days and reduced inventory levels from 60 days to 56 days. Finance growth from improving internal efficiencies rather than external debt.

Sound management indeed.

8.5.2   Using percentages

Some companies monitor working capital by relating the three main elements, accounts receivable, inventory and accounts payable as a percentage of sales rather than days.

Income Statement	Last Year		This Year		% Change
	Annual	Daily	Annual	Daily	
Sales revenue	R 365 000	R 1 000	R 401 500	R 1 100	10,00%
Cost of sales	R 255 500	R 700	R 281 050	R 770	10,00%
Balance sheet	Balance	Days	Balance	Days	
Accounts receivable	R 45 000	12,33%	R 47 350	11,79%	5,22%
Inventory	R 42 000	16,44%	R 43 500	15,48%	3,57%
Current assets	R 87 000		R 90 850		0,00%
Accounts payable	R 38 500	15,07%	R 42 350	15,07%	10,00%
Current liabilities	R 38 500		R 42 350	R 3 850	10,00%
Working capital	R 48 500		R 48 500	R -	0,00%

Again we can see that it is far easier to simply observe the resulting percentages to monitor our efficient management of working capital and cash.

Exercise 8. Impact on working capital

Mega Trading (Pty) Ltd is planning to increase sales by 15% next year. They expect debtor's days to increase by six days and inventory days to increase by nine days.

They plan to pay their suppliers within 45 days on average.

Given the data for this year in the table below, how much extra working capital, if any, will they require? Ignore the cash element of working capital.

The company works on a full calendar year of 365 trading days.

Income Statement	This Year		Next Year	
	Annual	Daily	Annual	Daily
Sales revenue	R 4 571 190,00	R 12 524,00		
Cost of sales	R 3 210 859,00	R 8 797,00		
Balance sheet	Balance	Days	Balance	Days
Accounts receivable	R 526 000,00	42		
Inventory	R 563 000,00	64		
Current assets	R 1 089 000,00	106		
Accounts payable	R 351 880,00	40		
Current liabilities	R 351 880,00	40		
Working capital	R 737 120,00			

Notes for my business plan

9   THE HIDDEN COST OF DISCOUNTS

Following on the above enlightenment, we can now discuss the impact of giving discounts to increase sales – a self-defeating objective if ever there was one.

Whilst discounting or reducing selling prices for special promotions is a perfectly sound strategy this section deals with unplanned discounting or "panic selling" if you like. It stems from the inability to set the correct value based price at the outset and/or the lack of selling skills to communicate said added value.

In the chase for revenue at all costs, sales people will be tempted to give away discounts to secure the business, spurred on by their sales revenue incentives and the sales manager's "KPIs".

A quick question but don't calculate the answer, just give your initial assessment. Here is the question:

Given a 20% gross profit margin, what percentage more do you think you must sell to maintain the gross profit value if a 7.5% discount is offered to your clients? Jot your answer down somewhere and we will come back to this little conundrum. Gut feel is what we are looking for.

9.1   Case study on discounts

Planet Earthmoving has set their budgets to achieve an operating profit of R25 000 000 with SG & A expenses of R90 000 000.

This is a tough market and margins are running at around 20%

They have set their sales targets accordingly and require R575 000 000 from the worldwide operations.

In case you forgot how we arrived at this figure:

a) operating profit (R25 000 000) + SG & A (R90 000 000)

= R115 000 000 contribution.

b) Contribution R115 000 000 ÷ 20% margin = R575 000 000 sales revenue.

In chasing this sales target, the sales people are buying business by giving their customers a 7.5% discount. What affect will this have on their carefully prepared budget?

To achieve the same operating profit, sales revenue must increase by 60%!

"Sixty percent increase in sales for just a 7.5% discount", you stammer.

The formula is quite simple. Here it is.

$$Sales\ increase = \frac{discount\ \%}{(\text{Original margin} - discount\ \%)}$$

$$Sales\ increase = \frac{7.5\%}{[20\% - 7.5\%]}$$

$\dfrac{7.5\%}{12.5\%} = 60\%$ increase in sales revenue

Which answer did you give?

9.2   Discounts change common size ratios

When you give discounts the common size (CS) ratios will change. Remember that:

cost of sales percentage + gross margin percentage = 100%.

If cost of sales is 80% then gross profit margin must equal 20%, 80% + 20% = 100%

After a 7.5% discount then:

Cost of sales (COS) = 80% + 7.5% = 87.5%

Gross profit margin = 20% -7 5% = 12.5%

	Before			After		
	Discount		CS %	7,50%		CS %
Revenue	R	10 000,00	100,00%	R	16 000,00	100,00%
COS	R	8 000,00	80,00%	R	14 000,00	87,50%
GP	R	2 000,00	20,00%	R	2 000,00	12,50%

Going back to Planet Earthmoving's problem we will see the impact on sales and working capital.

	Original Budget			Revised due to discounts		
Revenue	R	575 000 000	100,00%	R	920 000 000	100,00%
COS	R	460 000 000	80,00%	R	805 000 000	87,50%
Gross profit	R	115 000 000	20,00%	R	115 000 000	12,50%
SG & A expenses	R	90 000 000	15,65%	R	90 000 000	9,78%
Operating profit	R	25 000 000	4,35%	R	25 000 000	2,72%

We still need to make R115 000 000 gross profit to cover expenses and make the profit target but gross profit margin is now reduced to 12.5% from the original 20% after giving away the 7.5% discount.

But now the R115 000 000 is divided by only 12.5% gross profit margin requiring R920 000 000 in sales.

That is scary, really scary.

What happens when you see the sales target growing larger?

You chase those sales with even greater fervour and more frenzied discounts to "get the business" - and you go bust getting this business without even knowing why!

If the above is not enough to encourage you to sell margin rather than discounting then consider the further ramifications on the business. This is where the previous chapter on managing working capital plays a big role.

Let us examine what happens to accounts receivable, inventory, accounts payable and cash as they impact working capital.

We will assume for the exercise that the average accounts receivable days are 45. This means that you have an average of 45 days sales owing to the business.

Your planned AR (debtors) book is calculated as follows:

	Annual	Daily	AR days	AR Balance
Sales revenue	R 575 000 000	R 1 575 342	45	R 70 890 411

Let us now examine the new accounts receivable (debtors) balance based on the higher sales required due to discounting.

	Annual	Daily	AR Days	AR Balance
Actual actual	R 920 000 000	R 2 520 548	45	R 113 424 658
Planned sales	R 575 000 000	R 1 575 342	45	R 70 890 411
Variance	R 345 000 000	R 945 205		R 42 534 247

The accounts receivable balance has increased by R42 534 247

From your knowledge of working capital, you know that any increase in AR means a decrease in cash. So management has to scurry around funding this cash shortfall.

Can it get any worse you ask?

Yes.

Applying the same concepts to the inventory required to support the sales we will assume that your company carries sufficient inventory to cater for 60 days of sales. In other words, you hold 60 days x the daily COS figure.

	Annual	Daily	Inv Days	Inv Balance
Actual COS.	R 805 000 000	R 2 205 479	60	R 132 328 767
Planned COS	R 460 000 000	R 1 260 274	60	R 75 616 438
Variance	R 345 000 000	R 945 205		R 56 712 329

This will further reduce your cash flow by a staggering R56 712 329 as you need additional inventory to service the increased sales?

Is there no respite to this disaster?

Yes, a little.

The same adjustments must be made to accounts payable using the same rationale. Let us say that you pay your suppliers 42 days on average for purchases of inventory.

	Annual	Daily	AP Days	AP Balance
Actual COS	R 805 000 000	R 2 205 479	42	R 92 630 137
Planned COS	R 460 000 000	R 1 260 274	42	R 52 931 507
Variance	R 345 000 000	R 945 205		R 39 698 630

Your accounts payable (creditors) have increased by R39 698 630, and will improve the cash flow by the unpaid amount.

So the net impact on your cash flow is summarised as follows:

Changes to working capital from extra sales	Affect on Cash	
Increase in debtors or accounts receivable	R	(42 534 247)
Increase in inventory balance	R	(56 712 329)
Increase in accounts payable	R	39 698 630
Net impact on working capital and cash	R	(59 547 946)

So you are only down the tubes for a mere R60 000 000, give or take a few cents.

Now if interest rates are 10%, and you need an overdraft to finance this cash requirement, your interest costs would increase by about R6 000 000, which as you know, will further reduce profit before tax. To overcome this increased cost you will need to sell more, in fact R6 000 000 ÷ 12.5% (the new GP margin) which amounts to an additional R48 000 000 in sales.

What happens to accounts receivable, and inventory, and accounts payable, and cash, and interest expenses, as a result of the increased sales? We will not go there. I am sure that you have the message.

You need to be very careful in setting those all-important selling prices and be sure that the sales people are well trained in communicating the **added value** inherent in those all-important margins.

If cost savings are available through higher volume orders then indeed, pass those savings on to the customer but protect your margins.

Remember there are two selling prices – the highest and the lowest. The market sets the highest and the supplier sets the lowest. Cost plus pricing is really fantasy if it is over the market resistance level. The trick is where within that range do you price and why?

 Be sure that you can justify the added value in the business case and communicate it to the right people.

9.2 Discounting and the impact on ROWC

ROWC is the acronym for return on working capital. It is measured by expressing the operating profit as a percentage of the working capital.

$$ROWC = \frac{operating\ profit}{working\ capital}$$

Return on working capital measures the efficiency of managing working capital levels to support the level of sales.

Too much working capital lowers the efficiency of utilising these cash bound resources locked into debtors and inventory or even cash itself.

Too little working capital could lead to cash flow and liquidity problems. We need to get the balance right and monitor the trend against changing sales levels.

On the following pages we will examine the impact that lower selling prices have on this significant efficiency measure.

We will start a new page so that the table and explanation are on the same page for ease of reference. My pleasure.

a. Before the discount

The table below shows that return on working capital is an impressive 97.74%.

Before discount		
Selling price	R 100,00	
Cost price	R 65,00	
Sales revenue	R 200 000,00	CS%
Cost of sales	R 130 000,00	65,0%
Gross profit	R 70 000,00	35,0%
SG&A	R 38 000,00	19,0%
Operating profit	R 32 000,00	16,0%
		days
Accounts receivable	R 27 397,26	50,00
Inventory	R 26 712,33	75,00
Current assets	R 54 109,59	
Accounts payable	R 21 369,86	60,00
Current liabilities	R 21 369,86	
Working capital	R 32 739,73	65,00
ROWC	97,74%	
WC % of sales	16,37%	

Operating profit ÷ Working capital or

R32 000 ÷ R32 739.73 = 97.74%

The cash conversion days, or working capital days are 65 days:

AR days (50) + Inventory days (75) − AP days (60) = 65 days

and the working capital is 16.37% of the current sales amount:

R32 739.73 ÷ R200 000 = 16.37%

b. After the discount

Let's examine the results after dropping the selling price by 7.5%.

To compare apples with apples we have also maintained the same "days" relationship as before the discount. Accounts receivable days is still 50 days and inventory days remain at 75 days. Of course if sales increase significantly it is most likely that the "days" will also increase from the current scenario due to increased inefficiencies resulting from higher volumes within the same capacity.

After discount		Discount	Change
Discounted to S. Price	R 92,50	7,50%	
Cost price	R 65,00		
Sales revenue	R 254 545,45	CS%	27%
Cost of sales	R 184 545,45	72,5%	42%
Gross profit	R 70 000,00	27,5%	
SG&A	R 38 000,00	14,9%	
Operating profit	R 32 000,00	8,5%	-88%
Cash	Excluded	Days	Change
Accounts receivable	R 34 869,24	50,00	27%
Inventory	R 37 920,30	75,00	42%
Current assets	R 72 789,54		35%
Accounts payable	R 30 336,24	60,00	42%
Current liabilities	R 30 336,24		42%
Working capital (WC)	R 42 453,30	65,00	30%
Cash effect of change	-R 9 713,57		
ROWC	75,38%		-23%
WC % of sales	16,68%		

Whilst a 7.5% discount on a 35% gross profit margin does not seem much, the second table reflects the impact on company performance.

- Sales increase by 27% to compensate for the discount

- Operating profit return on sales drops by 88%

- Working capital increases by 30% or R9 713 which would negatively impact our cash

- ROWC drops by 23% from 97.74% to 75.38%

 Be wary of giving away margin as it may result in giving away your business.

Exercise 9. Effect of discounts on sales

Using the table below calculate the new sales revenue required for each of the two discount percentages allowed, 5% and 7.5% respectively.

Remember that the common size percentages will change due to the discounts. Refer back to page 58 if you are unsure about this.

Operating profit must remain at R426 865.

Commission is calculated on the new sales revenue amount, whilst the SG & A expenses maintain the original monetary value as shown. The SG & A percentage on sales will naturally change as will the operating profit percentage on sales.

		Discount allowed>>>>		5,00%	
			CS %	CS %	Amounts
Sales revenue	R 5 689 223	100%	100,00%		
Cost of sales	R 4 266 917	75,0%			
Gross profit	R 1 422 306	25,0%			
Commission	R 142 231	2,5%			
Contribution	R 1 280 075	22,5%			
SG & A expenses	R 853 210	15,0%		R 853 210	
Operating profit	R 426 865	7,5%		R 426 865	

		Discount allowed>>>>		7,50%	
			CS %	CS %	Amounts
Sales revenue	R 5 689 223	100%	100,00%		
Cost of sales	R 4 266 917	75,0%			
Gross profit	R 1 422 306	25,0%			
Commission	R 142 231	2,5%			
Contribution	R 1 280 075	22,5%			
SG & A expenses	R 853 210	15,0%		R 853 210	
Operating profit	R 426 865	7,5%		R 426 865	

Increase is calculated on the original sales revenue of R5 689 223.

Increased sales percentage for 5% discount is	%
Increased sales percentage for 7.5% discount is	%

Exercise 10. Effect of discounts on ROWC

Using the data in the table below calculate the working capital value before the discount is allowed. For the exercise you must now use **300** trading days (not 360 as we did before) to calculate the daily sales and daily cost of sales. Complete the exercise after the 7.5% discount is allowed and then complete the answers below:

	Before discount		After 7.5% discount		Change
	Amount	CS%	Amount	CS%	%
Sales revenue	R 570 000,00	100,0%		%	
Cost of sales	R 399 000,00	70,0%		%	
Gross profit	R 171 000,00	30,0%		%	
SG&A	R 38 000,00	6,7%		%	
Operating profit	R 133 000,00	23,3%	R 133 000,00	%	
		days		days	Change
Accounts receivable		50,00		50,00	
Inventory		75,00		75,00	
Current assets					
Accounts payable		60,00		60,00	
Current liabilities					
Working capital		65,00		65,00	
ROWC		%		%	
WC % of sales		%		%	

1	What is the new operating profit percentage or return on sales (ROS)?	%
2	How much more must we sell to make the same operating profit?	R
3	How much cash did the change in working capital require?	R
4	Calculate the ROWC after the discount.	%
5	Did the WC% of sales change significantly?	

Notes for my business plan

10 CHANGES IN EXPENSES

Business is not static. As managers you are called upon to keep abreast of ever changing situations and make changes in keeping with the profit targets set by management.

Costs change and these changes impact sales. You need to know what impact these changes have on changing the sales landscape. How much more must you sell to ensure extra costs are recovered and profits are not adversely affected. We need to address two issues:

- How much we must sell to maintain the operating profit or break even?

- How much more must we sell to maintain the return on sales efficiency ratio or percentage - ROS?

10.1 Breakeven – maintain operating profit value

Any change in fixed or SG & A expenses, requires a corresponding change in gross profit or contribution and any change in gross profit contribution requires a corresponding change in sales revenue.

Let us say that the SG & A expenses need to increase by R10 500. How much more must you sell to cover the increased expense and maintain the operating profit of R15 000 and so break-even?

	Amount	CS %
Revenue	R 100 000	100%
Cost of sales	R 65 000	65%
Gross profit	R 35 000	35%
2% commission	R 2 000	2%
Contribution	R 33 000	33%
SG & A expenses	R 18 000	18%
Operating profit	R 15 000	15%

REMEMBER: CS% is the common size percentage of any item expressed as a percentage of sales revenue.

It follows that, if expenses increase by R10 500, then contribution must also increase by R10 500.00 in order for the operating profit to remain as R15 000.00. Therefore, any increase in expenses must be covered by an equal increase in contribution to break even.

$$\frac{Contribution\ amount}{Contribution\ \%} = sales\ revenue$$

and to break even, the increased expense requires the same increase in contribution or gross profit. You can therefore simply divide the increased expense by the contribution percentage to arrive at the extra revenue required to cover the extra expense.

$$extra\ revenue = \frac{expense\ increase}{contribution\ \%}$$

$$\frac{R10\ 500}{33\%} = R31\ 818.18$$

and your income statement would now reflect the new figures as follows:

	Amount	CS %	Change	Total	CS %
Revenue	R 100 000	100%	R 31 818	R 131 818	100%
Cost of sales	R 65 000	65%	R 20 682	R 85 682	65%
Gross profit	R 35 000	35%	R 11 136	R 46 136	35%
2% commission	R 2 000	2%	R 636	R 2 636	2%
Contribution	R 33 000	33%	R 10 500	R 43 500	33%
SG & A expenses	R 18 000	18%	R 10 500	R 28 500	22%
Operating profit	R 15 000	15%	R -	R 15 000	11%

So your contribution has increased by the R10 500 which you required to cover the increased expense of R10 500. You have also maintained your profit of R15 000. The fact that your profit has remained unchanged means that you have **broken even**.

Note that your profit in relation to revenue has declined from 15% to 11% which means that your efficiency has declined. Expenses have increased in relation to sales generated.

After the next practice exercise we will attempt to solve this problem.

Exercise 11.   how much must we sell to break even?

		Original	Common Size%
Revenue	R	385 000,00	100,00%
COS	R	261 800,00	68,00%
Gross profit	**R**	**123 200,00**	**32,00%**
Commission	R	7 700,00	2,00%
Contribution	**R**	**115 500,00**	**30,00%**
Advertising	R	2 865,00	0,74%
Bank charges	R	1 389,00	0,36%
Rent	R	5 500,00	1,43%
Wages	R	32 000,00	8,31%
Depreciation	R	6 500,00	1,69%
Salaries	R	26 530,00	6,89%
Operating profit	**R**	**40 716,00**	**10,58%**
Interest expense	R	1 668,00	0,43%
Other income	R	4 000,00	1,04%
NIBT	**R**	**43 048,00**	**11,18%**
Tax	R	12 914,40	3,35%
Net income	**R**	**30 133,60**	**7,83%**

Salaries are expected to increase by 8% next year and wages by 8.5%.Using the data from this income statement, please answer the following questions

1	Complete an income statement showing the new data.	
2	How much **more** must you sell to cover the increased expenses, and maintain the current operating profit?	R
3	You are now told that due to tighter trading conditions the gross profit percentage will drop to 30% next year. Given the same wage and salary increases, how much more must you sell to maintain the current operating profit?	R

10.2 Expenses change - maintaining ROS %?

You learnt from the earlier exercise that, whilst the breakeven calculation will accurately calculate the extra sales just to cover the extra expenses, because the sales value is increased and the operating profit remains unchanged, the ratio of operating profit to sales revenue (ROS) naturally decreases. Same operating profit expressed as a percentage of the higher sales revenue. See P69.

Before   R15 000 ÷ R100 000 = 15.00% ROS

After R15 000 ÷ R131 818 = 11.34%

If the company wanted to **maintain the profit efficiency ratio** to sales, how much more must it sell to cover the new fixed costs, or new profit target, and **maintain the return on sales percentage?**

Remember that your task is to determine how much extra revenue is required to cover any extra fixed costs without any decrease to the operating profit percentage of sales efficiency measure.

This is a bit tricky so you may want to check the sprinklers or change your drink before tackling it.

Time to focus.

We will use the following income statement for this exercise:

	Amount	CS%
Revenue	R 285 000	100,00%
COS	R 193 800	68,00%
Gross profit	R 91 200	32,00%
Commission	R 5 700	2,00%
Contribution	R 85 500	30,00%
Advertising	R 2 865	1,01%
Bank charges	R 1 389	0,49%
Rent	R 5 500	1,93%
Salaries	R 26 530	9,31%
Operating profit	R 49 216	17,27%
Interest expense	R 1 668	0,59%
Other Income	R 4 000	1,40%
NIBT	R 51 548	18,09%
Tax	R 15 464	5,43%
Net income	R 36 084	12,66%

You are unsuccessful in the wage negotiation and are forced to increase the salaries expense by R3 550.

How much more must you sell to cover this increase and maintain the current operating return on sales (ROS) which is 17.27%?

 The common size percentages hold the key.

If you know the relationship between the fixed expenses (SG&A expenses) and the sales revenue then once again you have an easy way of solving the problem. By adding the common size percentages of all the fixed expenses you arrive at:

1.01% + .49% + 1.93% + 9.31% = 12.73%.

The fixed expense element of the income statement therefore represents 12.73% of sales revenue. You can test this another way:

R2 865 + R1 389 + R5 500 + R26 530 = R36 284 which is 12.73% of sales revenue.

The additional revenue is calculated by dividing the extra expense by the **total expense common size percentage.** We will label this the **TECS%.**

$$\frac{R3\,550}{12.73\%} = R27\,887\ \textit{additional sales}$$

Our income statement now reflects the changes as follows:

		Amount	CS%	Change		New Total		CS %
Revenue	R	285 000	100,0%	R	27 887	R	312 887	100,0%
COS	R	193 800	68,0%	R	18 963	R	212 763	68,0%
Gross profit	**R**	**91 200**	**32,0%**	**R**	**8 924**	**R**	**100 124**	**32,0%**
Commission	R	5 700	2,0%	R	558	R	6 258	2,0%
Contribution	**R**	**85 500**	**30,0%**	**R**	**8 366**	**R**	**93 866**	**30,0%**
Advertising	R	2 865	1,0%	R	-	R	2 865	0,9%
Bank charges	R	1 389	0,5%	R	-	R	1 389	0,4%
Rent	R	5 500	1,9%	R	-	R	5 500	1,8%
Salaries	R	26 530	9,3%	R	3 550	R	30 080	9,6%
Operating profit	**R**	**49 216**	**17,3%**	**R**	**4 816**	**R**	**54 032**	**17,3%**
Interest expense	R	1 668	0,6%	R	-	R	1 668	0,5%
Other Income	R	4 000	1,4%	R	-	R	4 000	1,3%
NIBT	**R**	**51 548**	**18,1%**	**R**	**4 816**	**R**	**56 364**	**18,0%**
Tax	R	15 464	5,4%	R	1 445	R	16 909	5,4%
Net income	**R**	**36 084**	**12,7%**	**R**	**3 371**	**R**	**39 455**	**12,6%**

You have now increased sales by enough to cover the increased expense as well as maintaining the operating profit ROS percentage of 17.27% on the new sales figure of R312 887.

Imagine sitting in the planning meeting and your manager suggests that some expense needs to be increased for whatever reason and you immediately come back with the question;

"Can we sell an extra R27 887 to pay for this increase sir?" (I added the sir to speed up your promotion path).

And the rest of the team are gobsmacked as you visualise your new position and the changes you will make as manager.

But what if you have 20 items on the income statement and need to add all 20 percentages together? Heavy PT.

TIP

The difference between the contribution percentage and the operating profit percentage represents the total costs between these two line items expressed as a percentage.

74

In the next example this is:

*TECS% = 30% contribution – 17.27% operating profit

*TECS% = 12.73%

*TECS is **T**otal **E**xpense **C**ommon Size

		Amount	CS%		
Revenue	R	285 000	100,00%		
COS	R	193 800	68,00%		
Gross profit	**R**	**91 200**	**32,00%**		
Commission	R	5 700	2,00%		
Contribution	**R**	**85 500**	**30,00%**	30,00%	
Advertising	R	2 865	1,01%		
Bank charges	R	1 389	0,49%	12,73%	
Rent	R	5 500	1,93%		
Salaries	R	26 530	9,31%		
Operating profit	**R**	**49 216**	**17,27%**	17,27%	
Interest expense	R	1 668	0,59%		
Other income	R	4 000	1,40%		
NIBT	**R**	**51 548**	**18,09%**		
Tax	R	15 464	5,43%		
Net income	**R**	**36 083,60**	**12,66%**		

So we can now formulate our formula as follows:

$$\frac{Increased\ expense}{TECS\%} = \textit{extra sales to maintain ROS\%}$$

Exercise 12.   Expenses change –maintain the ROS%?

		Amount	CS%
Revenue	R	414 500	100,00%
COS	R	281 860	68,00%
Gross profit	R	**132 640**	**32,00%**
Commission	R	8 290	2,00%
Contribution	R	**124 350**	**30,00%**
Advertising	R	3 522	0,85%
Bank charges	R	1 895	0,46%
Rent	R	7 825	1,89%
Salaries	R	35 886	8,66%
Operating profit	R	**75 222**	**18,15%**
Interest expense	R	2 136	0,52%
Other income	R	5 200	1,25%
NIBT	R	**78 286**	**18,89%**
Tax	R	23 486	5,67%
Net income	R	**54 800,20**	**13,22%**

Salaries are expected to increase by 8% next year and wages by 8.5%.Using the data from this income statement, please answer the following questions

1	How much **more** must you sell to cover the increased expenses, and maintain the current operating profit?	R
2	You are now told that due to tighter trading conditions the gross profit percentage will drop to 30% next year. Given the same wage and salary increases, how much more must you sell to maintain the current operating profit?	R

We will now explore some variations on this theme.

10.2.1 Variation 1 – maintaining net income percentage of sales

The analytically observant amongst us have immediately detected that as a result your net income before tax (NIBT) and net income after tax have now changed the common size percentage to revenue (see previous table). The operating efficiency as measured by the net income ROS % has decreased from 12.66% to 12.61%!

What do we do?

Before tackling this problem we need to explain the relationship between NIBT and net income.

As you have a relationship between revenue, cost of sales and gross profit (contribution) so too the same relationship exists between NIBT, tax and net income.

Net income before tax	100%	R 100 000,00	Sales
Tax at the rate of...	30%	R 30 000,00	COS
Net income after tax	70%	R 70 000,00	GP

If the net income target is R25 000 then the NIBT amount must be:

$$\frac{net\ income}{(1 - tax\ rate)} = net\ income\ before\ tax$$

If net income after tax needs to be R25 000 then NIBT will be:

$$\frac{R25\ 000}{(100\% - tax\ rate\ \%)}$$

$$\frac{R25\ 000}{(100\% - 30\%)} = R35\ 714.28$$

TIP   *As long as the NIBT percentage of sales is maintained the resulting net income after tax percentage of sales will also be achieved.*

To maintain the NIBT percentage, and therefore the net income percentage, you simply change the TECS% calculation to include these other elements.

Going back to the original income statement where the original revenue amount was R285 500 you now subtract the NIBT percentage from the contribution percentage to arrive at the TECS%.

TECS% = 30.00% - 18.09% = 11.91%

The extra revenue to cover the increase of R3 550.00 is calculated as:

$$\frac{R3\,550}{11.91\%} = R29\,806 \; extra \; sales \; revenue$$

New total revenue is R314 807.

Time to check our results on the income statement.

	Original	CS %	Change		Revised	CS %
Revenue	R 285 000	100,00%	R 29 807	R 314 807	100,00%
COS	R 193 800	68,00%	R 20 269	R 214 069	68,00%
Gross profit	R 91 200	32,00%	R 9 538	R 100 738	32,00%
Commission	R 5 700	2,00%	R 596	R 6 296	2,00%
Contribution	R 85 500	30,00%	R 8 942	R 94 442	30,00%
Advertising	R 2 865	1,01%	R -	R 2 865	0,91%
Bank charges	R 1 389	0,49%	R -	R 1 389	0,44%
Rent	R 5 500	1,93%	R -	R 5 500	1,75%
Salaries	R 26 530	9,31%	R 3 550	R 30 080	9,56%
Operating profit	R 49 216	17,27%	R 5 392	R 54 608	17,35%
Interest expense	R 1 668	0,59%	R -	R 1 668	0,53%
Other income	R 4 000	1,40%	R -	R 4 000	1,27%
NIBT	R 51 548	18,09%	R 5 392	R 56 940	18,09%
Tax	R 15 464	5,43%	R 1 618	R 17 082	5,43%
Net income	R 36 084	12,66%	R 3 774	R 39 858	12,66%

The NIBT percentage and the net income percentage have remained as they were before the salaries increase. We have now covered the extra cost and maintained the net income return on sales percentage.

It's all about understanding those common size percentages to unlock the secrets of the income statement

10.2.2 Variation 2 - contribution percent changes

What happens if the contribution percentage will change next year?

Using our example the contribution percentage goes from 30% to 28% but NIBT must remain at 18.09%. Of course we would not be so meticulous as to have 18.09% but we will just stay with the example we are using.

TECS% will now be the difference between the new contribution common size percentage and the existing profit line common size percentage.

TECS% = 28% - 18.09%

TECS% = 9.91%

$$\frac{R3\,550}{9.91\%} = R35\,822 \; additional \; sales$$

10.2.3 Variation 3 - change in tax rate

What happens if the tax rate changes and you need to maintain the after tax net income ROS efficiency?

We just need to adjust the TECS% based on the revised NIBT percent required and then divide the total costs by the new TECS%.

We will assume that the new tax rate is now 35%. So if tax rate is 35% then Net income after tax = 100% - 35% = 65%.

Old	New
18,09%	19,48%
30,00%	35,00%
12,66%	12,66%

If tax rate is 35% and the required net income after tax is 12.66% we can calculate the common size percentage for the NIBT as follows:

$$NIBT\% = \frac{\text{net income ROS\%}}{(1 - \text{tax rate})}$$

$$NIBT\% = \frac{12.66\%}{(100\% - 35\%)}$$

$$NIBT\% = \frac{12.66\%}{65\%}$$

$$New\ NIBT\% = 19.48\%\ \text{of sales}$$

What do we know so far?

- Net income after tax must be 12.66% of sales

- Tax rate is now 35%

- NIBT CS% is 19.48% of sales

- Contribution percentage is 30% of sales

- Net total expenses and other income is the difference between the contribution and NIBT values:

- R85 500 – R51 548 = R33 952

- TECS% is now (30% - 19.48%) (Contribution % - NIBT %)

- TECS% = 10.52%

$$Sales\ revenue = \frac{\text{net total expenses}}{\text{TECS}\%}$$

$$Sales\ revenue = \frac{\text{R33 952}}{10.52\%}$$

$$Sales\ revenue = R322\ 737$$

Once again by understanding the simple relationship between income statement values and their common size percentages relationship to sales we can easily calculate the sales amount required to cover the new changes

We will check this result on the following income statement:

		Original	CS %		Revised	CS %
Revenue	R	285 000	100,00%	R	322 738	100,00%
COS	R	193 800	68,00%	R	219 462	68,00%
Gross profit	R	91 200	32,00%	R	103 276	32,00%
Commission	R	5 700	2,00%	R	6 455	2,00%
Contribution	R	85 500	30,00%	R	96 821	30,00%
Advertising	R	2 865	1,01%	R	2 865	0,89%
Bank charges	R	1 389	0,49%	R	1 389	0,43%
Rent	R	5 500	1,93%	R	5 500	1,70%
Salaries	R	26 530	9,31%	R	26 530	8,22%
Operating profit	R	49 216	17,27%	R	60 537	18,76%
Interest expense	R	1 668	0,59%	R	1 668	0,52%
Other income	R	4 000	1,40%	R	4 000	1,24%
NIBT	R	51 548	18,09%	R	62 869	19,48%
Tax	R	15 464	5,43%	R	22 004	6,82%
Net income	R	36 084	12,66%	R	40 865	12,66%

10.2.4   Variation 4 - new budgets with no history

You are preparing a new budget and have no historical sales revenue figure upon which to calculate common size percentages. The only information you have is the following:

- We expect to make 30% gross profit

- The tax rate will be 28%

- Sales commission will be 2.5% of revenue

- Total fixed costs will be R1 650 000

- Management require a net income after tax of 9%

How much must we sell?

Impossible to compute you say! Let's see how we go about this.

This is the ham sandwich approach as we will start at each end of the income statement and work towards the middle. Again, you will work with the percentages that reflect the relationship between these activities.

We will start a new page to get everything in one place.

Please refer to the steps numbered under the "method" column to populate the spreadsheet.

The target profit is now the NIBT % which we need to calculate.

	% of NIBT	Amount	Common Size %	Step	Method
Sales revenue			100,00%	9	Calculated
COS			70,00%	2	Calculated
Gross profit			30,00%	1	Given
Commission			2,50%	3	Given
Contribution			27,50%	4	Calculated
Fixed costs		R 1 650 000	15,00%	8	Calculated
Operating profit					
Interest expense					
NIBT	100%		12,50%	7	Calculated
Tax	28%	Given	3,50%	6	Calculated
Net Income After Tax	72%	Calculated	9,00%	5	Given

1. The gross profit percentage is given as being 30%

2. Cost of sales percentage is calculated as: 100% - GP%= 70%

3. The commission percentage is given as being 2.5%

4. The contribution percentage is the GP percentage - commission percentage

    30% - 2.5% = 27.50%

We will now go to the bottom of the income statement to fill in other clues.

5. Net income after tax percentage required is 9%

6. If the tax rate is 28% then..

7. The NIBT can be calculated as 9% ÷ 72% = 12.5%. Remember that if the tax rate is 28% of NIBT then net income after tax must be 72% of NIBT. Net income after tax + tax = Net income before tax.

8. Fixed costs value given as R1 650 000.

We know that Total Expense Common Size, or TECS, percentage is the difference between contribution percentage and NIBT %

TECS% is now 27.50% contribution - 12.5% NIBT = 15%

9. Sales revenue is calculated by dividing the known fixed costs amount by the calculated TECS%

$$\frac{R1\ 650\ 000}{15\%} = R11\ 000\ 000$$

The income statement will reflect the result as follows:

		Amount	CS %
Sales revenue	R	11 000 000	100,00%
COS	R	7 700 000	70,00%
Gross profit	R	3 300 000	30,00%
Sales commission	R	275 000	2,50%
Contribution	R	3 025 000	27,50%
Expenses	R	1 650 000	15,00%
Operating profit	R	1 375 000	12,50%
Interest costs	R	-	
NIBT	R	1 375 000	12,50%
Tax	R	385 000	3,50%
Net income	R	990 000	9,00%

Problem solved!

Being forever vigilant, you immediately noted that the expense is 15% of sales, which is the same as the TECS% that you calculated.

 Common size percentages take the guess work out of planning.

10.2.5 Variation 5 – other income and interest expense

Following on variation 4 where we only had fixed expenses and the common size percentages, our problem is further complicated by having to account for expenses and income after the operating profit. How do we calculate sales targets to allow for these items as well?

	% of NIBT	Amount	Common Size %	Step	Method
Sales revenue			100,00%	9	Calculated
COS			70,00%	2	Calculated
Gross profit			30,00%	1	Calculated
Commission			2,50%	3	Given
Contribution			27,50%	4	Calculated
Fixed costs		R 1 650 000	15,00%	8	Calculated
Operating profit					
Interest expense		R -100 000			
Other income		R 500 000			
NIBT	100%		12,50%	7	Calculated
Tax	28%	Given	3,50%	6	Calculated
Net Income After Tax	72%	Calculated	9,00%	5	Given

Steps 1 to 8 in variation 4 which we just covered remain as they are.

Now we need to account for other income and expenses. Calculate net adjusted amount as follows:

- Fixed costs + other expenses – other income

- R1 650 000 + R100 000 – R500 000 = R1 250 00

Sales revenue is calculated by dividing net adjusted amount by the TECS%:

$$\frac{R1\,250\,000}{12.5\%} = R8\,333\,333$$

The income statement will reflect the result as follows:

	Amount	CS %	Result	
Sales revenue		100,00%	R 8 333 333	100,00%
COS		72,00%	R 5 833 333	70,00%
Gross profit		28,00%	R 2 500 000	30,00%
Commission		2,50%	R 208 333	2,50%
Contribution		25,50%	R 2 291 667	27,50%
Fixed costs	R 1 650 000	13,00%	R 1 650 000	19,80%
Operating profit			R 641 667	7,70%
Interest expense	-R 100 000		-R 100 000	-1,20%
Other income	R 500 000		R 500 000	6,00%
NIBT	100%	12,50%	R 1 041 667	12,50%
Tax	28%		-R 291 667	-3,50%
Net Income After Tax	72%	9,00%	R 750 000	9,00%

I hope you will find these exercises useful in your decision making and budgeting to maintain the wealth and efficiencies in your business. The methodology provides a quick solution to the question, "How much extra must you sell to cover additional expenses and maintain your ROS percentage efficiency?"

You could of course run many iterations of the income statement, but this gets the solution within seconds.

11 MEETING SHAREHOLDERS' EXPECTATIONS

Finally, we look at how we link shareholder requirements to sales targets.

 Remember that this is why we are in business

There are three ratios we will to focus on:

- Earnings per share (EPS)

- Return on equity (ROE)

- Return on investment (ROI)

They all have one thing in common – profit or earnings, not revenue!

The objective of this session is to build on the processes we have already covered to answer these questions:

1. If we need to increase the EPS by 15%, how much must we sell?
2. If ROE needs to be 50% above inflation, how much must we sell?
3. If we are targeting an ROI of 18%, how much must we sell?

The methodology is the same for all three questions but the starting point varies for each.

11.1 Earnings per share (EPS)

EPS is the net income after tax divided by the number of ordinary shares issued. If there are 2 000 000 shares issued and the net income after tax is R400 000 then the EPS is;

$$EPS = \frac{R400\ 000}{2\ 000\ 000} = R0.20\ EPS$$

If we needed to increase the EPS to R0.25 then the net income after tax would need to increase to:

2 000 000 shares x R0.25cents = R500 000 net income

11.2 Return on equity (ROE)

ROE is the net income after tax expressed as a percentage of the equity invested by the owners.

Assuming a total investment in the company of R5 500 000 of which the owners' portion or owners' equity, is R2 500 000. The balance of the investment is funded from debt of R3 000 000.

Staying with our net income of R400 000 we can calculate the ROE as being:

$$ROE = \frac{R400\ 000}{R2\ 500\ 000} = 16\%\ ROE$$

The equity is found on the balance sheet under non-current liabilities. If no further shares were issued and we wanted to increase ROE to 25% the net income would need to be R625 000.

R2 500 000 x 25% = R625 000

11.3 Return on investment (ROI)

ROI is the net income after tax expressed as a percentage of the total funds invested in the business.

In our example the total investment is R5 500 000 of which

R2 500 000 is funded by the owners and R3 000 000 by borrowings or debt.

In order to achieve a ROI of 12.5%, we would require a net profit of:

R5 500 000 x 12.5% = R687 500

11.4 Process

By achieving the highest net income we will cover all three requirements. In this case the highest net income target is that required for ROI – R687 000.

Other data given for the budgeting exercise are as follows.

- The tax rate is 30%

- Gross profit margins average 28%

- Commission is 2% of sales

- Their debt financing cost is R200 000, that is the interest expense

- SG&A expenses (fixed costs) are R15 000 000 per annum

How much must they sell to meet all three targets?

For this exercise we will turn the income statement upside down and start with net income at the top and work down to the sales revenue target at the bottom.

Step		Data	Values
1	Net income after tax	70,0%	R 687 000
2	Tax rate	30,0%	
3	Net income before tax		R 981 429
4	Interest expense		R 200 000
5	Operating profit		R 1 181 429
6	SG&A expenses		R 9 500 000
7	Contribution	26,0%	R 10 681 429
8	Sales revenue	100,0%	R 41 082 418

A different approach but really quite logical and it places emphasis on the top line which becomes profit, not sales.

1. Enter the net income

2. Enter tax rate as given

3. Calculate NIBT which is the net income ÷ 70% (1 − Tax rate)

4. Enter interest expense which is given

5. Add NIBT and interest expense to arrive at operating profit

6. Enter SG&A expenses of R9 500 000

7. Add SG&A expenses to operating profit to arrive at contribution.

8. Divide contribution by contribution % = sales revenue

Time to prove it by producing our conventional income statement as follows:

Sales revenue	R	41 082 418	100,0%
Cost of sales	R	29 579 341	72,0%
Gross profit	R	11 503 077	28,0%
Commission	R	821 648	2,0%
Contribution	R	10 681 429	26,0%
SG&A expenses	R	9 500 000	23,1%
Operating profit	R	1 181 429	2,9%
Interest expense	R	200 000	0,5%
NIBT	R	981 429	2,4%
Tax 30%	R	294 429	0,7%
Net income after tax	R	687 000	1,7%

Voila! And there you have it.

Not sure if the shareholders will be to impressed by these figures. Only 1.7% return on sales! Better check the detail of those SG & A expenses.

Exercise 13.   Meeting shareholder expectations

The board has reviewed the year ahead and decided to increase shareholder returns by 20% and also ensure that the ROI is 25% greater than the prevailing inflation rate of 8%. There are 10 000 000 shares and last year the earnings per share was 20cents.

The business is funded through R9 000 000 from shareholders' equity plus R6 000 000 interest bearing debt and R8 000 000 non-interest bearing debt.

SG&A expenses are expected to be R8 650 000 for the year and borrowing costs will be 10% of the interest bearing value.

The market is tough and trading conditions are pushing margins down to a budgeted 20% gross profit. Commission on sales is 2.5% and the corporate tax rate is 29%.

Step		Data	Values	CS%
1	Net income after tax			
	Tax rate			
2	Net income before tax			
	Interest expense			
3	Operating profit			
	SG&A expenses			
4	Contribution			
7	Commission			
	Gross profit			
6	Cost of sales			
5	**Sales revenue**			

Notes for my business plan

12 OPERATIONAL BUDGETING

12.1 What is a budget?

Whether you are planning for your personal wealth creation or the wealth creation of a business, the objective is to maximise the returns you get on the funds and resources available to us as individuals or to the business entity.

You may simplify these resources as being:

- Moments (time)

- Money

- Manpower

- Machines

The overriding question to be asked is ...

"How can I maximise my return on these scarce resources?"

You need to examine the economy, the market, the competition, your resources and anything else relevant to making a success of the time and money you will be investing to achieve the objectives.

To arrive at the answers requires thinking, discussing, debating, arguing, brainstorming, employing consultants and any other cost effective resource to come up with the most viable plan.

 You may want to invite important customers and suppliers as well.

Having finalised your strategies, tactics and activities you need to reduce these words and assumptions to a meaningful and understandable format to keep everyone on track with all the clever thinking that resulted in the final plan.

The budget is the tool that reduces all the planning and thinking and debating and evaluating and scenario analysis to monetary expressions of your final decisions on how you will achieve the objectives you have set or have been set.

A budget is simply the plans and costs of those plans to generate a required amount of profit and cash from the business and/or to achieve a required growth in sales revenue in line with company objectives.

It is the business plan for success set out in money terms phased over a period of time.

12.2 Where do you start with your budget?

Well that depends on where you are in the budgeting hierarchy.

At executive level you will probably start with how you plan to increase the wealth of the shareholders or owners.

This may be in terms of earnings per share, increase in the share price, return on equity, return on investment, dividend policy or any of the measurements you might be using to achieve your corporate objectives.

At a business unit level you will probably be given some directives from executive level such as increase operating profit (aka PBIT or EBIT) by 15% with revenue increase of 10% and return on sales of 16%.

At a cost centre level you may simply be budgeting within a total cost parameter that says your total costs should not be greater than R1 000 000 for the year or 10% over the previous year.

At a sales management level you may be told to increase sales revenue by 12% whilst maintaining a GP margin of 28% and the selling costs of sales people and promotional activities to be kept to 5% of total revenue.

In a manufacturing environment you may be advised to keep inventories to 40 days and reduce manufacturing lead times by 20%.

The fact of the matter is that the budget is very seldom an open-ended plan without constraints from some higher level and your job is to make it work within those constraints.

The reason you are employed is to bring your skills, knowledge, experience, applied learning and intelligence to the party to achieve those objectives. You are acting on behalf of the owners to achieve the objectives of wealth creation for which you are remunerated.

Hopefully you will be involved in pre-budget discussions with management for them to hear your input before final decisions are made.

12.3 Gaining budget approval

To gain budget approval, managers will often ignore other ancillary costs linked to an expense.

You will typically find a situation where two additional people are requested at say R15 000 basic salary each but no provisions are made for additional office space, teas and coffees, parking facilities, telephone costs, training costs, year-end conference costs, stationary costs, extra software licences for PC's, additional network costs for connecting them to the system, ADSL lines, additional office furniture and so on.

In fact you may even see the budget for these items reduced in an attempt to offset the costs of employing these extra people and balance the budget.

So you submit this unrealistic budget to management who, would you believe, are actually as aware of these other extra costs as you are, and then you wonder why the budget is rejected.

And so you waste more time in redoing the budget and the world is moving on.

Managers often get frustrated, dejected and demotivated when their budget is changed by their manager but when you examine your budget proposal carefully, you will discover that you would probably have done the same thing if you were that manager.

A line manager submits a request for budget to employ an extra technician for R15 000 per month total cost to company. The reason given simply states that you need an extra man to service your customers.

This is seen as a cost by management, and costs reduce profit!

If the manager motivated the request by justifying it in terms of investing to maintain, or increase, revenue flows by retaining customers then they will have a better chance.

How about this approach?

"Due to increasing travel delays in the urban area of Pretoria caused by road construction, our average response times to service major customers has dropped from 1.25 hours to 2.15 hours. This has caused Nedbank and Anglo to send letters of complaint to your branch and copies to you.

As you aware these accounts are under perpetual threat from opposition and decreasing service delivery puts these R30 000 000 accounts at risk.

In addition, Mike Jones will be retiring in two years and I need to get his knowledge transferred to new technicians.

I have considered all alternatives with my team and believe this investment of R180 000pa to protect this income stream to be the most cost effective solution."

Always remember that there is only a limited pot of funding available to all managers and the money goes where the return is best. Protecting investments is more attractive than increasing costs!

Place yourself in your manager's position when reviewing your budget request and ask yourself how you would react. Then redo your request.

12.4 Preparing the groundwork

It is always a good idea to make a note of how you calculated each line item of your budget. It supports your reasoning and helps you to refer back when thing go wrong later on in the year. You will have a record of how you arrived at the figures and will be able to explain variances from the original plan.

Last Year Actual			Next Year Budget			Changes in Budget
10 000 000	% of	1	Existing Income	10 850 000	% of	8,50%
600 000	income	2	New income	660 000	Income	10,00%
10 600 000	**100,00%**		**Total income**	**11 510 000**	**100,00%**	**8,58%**
636 000	6,00%	3	Administration costs	735 000	6,39%	16%
159 000	1,50%	4	Audit fees	65 000	0,56%	-59%
79 500	0,75%	5	Bank charges	63 500	0,55%	-20%
265 000	2,50%	6	Depreciation	301 000	2,62%	14%
901 000	8,50%	7	Electricity	11 265 000	10,62%	1150%
2 120 000	20,00%	8	Salaries	2 070 180	17,99%	-2%
1 590 000	15,00%	9	Maintenance	1 899 150	16,50%	19%
75 260	0,71%	10	Petrol	80 986	0,70%	8%
1 908 000	18,00%	11	Wages	1 930 896	16,78%	1%
689 000	6,50%	12	Property Rates & taxes	757 900	7,05%	10,00%
8 422 760	**79,46%**		**Total expenses**	**9 180 388**	**79,76%**	**9,00%**
2 177 240	**20,54%**		**Operating profit**	**2 329 612**	**20,24%**	**7,00%**

Salaries		Notes	Notes to 2010 Budget			
Headcount	180	1	Existing Income ispror year actual adjusted by 8.5% inflation			
Income per head	11 778	2	10% Increase on due to depressed market conditions			
Wages						
Headcount	350	3	New FICA requirements and expected to increase this cost			
Income per head	5 451	4	Change in external audit requirements should reduce audit costs			
		5	Increased internet banking and new client EFT and supplier payment system			
		6	Previous year actual + 20% on new R 180 000 panel van			
		7	Prior year cost to income, R901 000+ 25% increase R225 250			
		8	Salary calculations			
		8a	Headcount		162	Reduce headcount by 10%
		8b	Income per head	R	12 778,89	Increase per head 8.5%
		9	Increased costs based on new maintenance contracts with contractors			
		10	Based on 4 panel vans x 1 850 lpm@ 10l per 100km @ R 9.12/litre			
		11	Wages calculation			
		11a	Headcount		322	Reduce headcount by 8%
		11b	Income per head	R	5 996,57	Increase per head 10%
		12	Prior year + 10% increase			

12.5 Analysing the variances

Having done the preparation thoroughly it is now much easier to provide management, and yourself, with the reasons why business is deviating from the plan. You can summarise these reasons under two headings:

1. Reasons under your control – staff performance, equipment failure, etc.

2. Reasons beyond your control – petrol price increase, exchange rate collapse, government interventions and the like.

		YYYY Budget		Actual		Change on Budget	% Change
1	Existing Income	10 850 000	% of	10 705 000	% of	-145 000	-1,34%
2	New income	660 000	Income	613 500	Income	-46 500	-7,05%
	Total income	11 510 000	1581,04%	11 318 500	1554,74%	-191 500	-1,66%
3	Administration Costs	735 000	100,96%	728 000	4682457,92%	7 000	0,95%
4	Audit fees	65 000	8,93%	86 500	11,88%	-21 500	-33,08%
5	Bank charges	63 500	8,72%	70 200	9,64%	-6 700	-10,55%
6	Depreciation	301 000	41,35%	302 566	41,56%	-1 566	-0,52%
7	Electricity	1 222 934	167,99%	1 203 661	165,34%	19 273	1,58%
8	Salaries	2 070 180	284,37%	2 156 630	296,24%	-86 450	-4,18%
9	Maintenance	1 899 150	260,87%	1 750 000	240,38%	149 150	7,85%
10	Petrol	80 995	11,13%	82 566	11,34%	-1 571	-1,94%
11	Wages	1 930 896	265,23%	1 998 750	274,55%	-67 854	-3,51%
12	COJ Rates	811 743	111,50%	809 556	111,20%	2 187	0,27%
	Total expenses	9 180 398	1261,04%	9 188 429	81,18%	-8 031	-0,09%
	Operating profit	2 329 602	320,00%	2 130 071	1473,56%	-183 469	-7,88%

Notes	Reasons for variance			
1	Rental increase on Block A was delayed by 1 month as owner in hospital R 48 000			
2	93% of new business target achieved. 2 senior sales people left and increased competition from A - Z Rentals			
3	Within acceptable limits			
4	Underestimated costs of changing to new sself audit system. Required additionsl year end help			
5	IT Installation delayed by 3 months so lost the benefit of the reduced fees			
6	Within acceptable limits			
7	Increases came in on time as expected but extra savings due to Solar panels installed 2009			
8	Salary calculations			
8a	Headcount		168	Could not reduce to 162 due to audit problems
8b	Income per head	R	12 837,00	Budgeted on R 12 778. R 59.00 per head
9	Less maintenance than 2009.			
10	Increase in fuel price of 2.55 over budget offset by reduced mileage travelled			
11	Wages calculation			
11a	Headcount		330	Could only reduce by 20 due to union threats
11b	Income per head	R	6 056,82	Final increase was 11%
12	Within acceptable limits			

Variance analysis should be done immediately when the actuals are produced in order to feed the business plan with the required changes to bring the plan back on track.

Budgeting is a most critical area of any business as management will determine cash requirements and other resources required to meet the plan their managers have set for achieving the overall objective of meeting shareholders' expectations. This leads to our next section.

12.6 Bonuses and budgets

Many companies still offer attractive bonuses for over achieving profit targets which in itself causes problems. If managers can earn large bonuses for over achieving the profit targets then one needs to ask the obvious question.

Will their focus be more on achieving shareholder expectations or on over achieving the target for bigger bonus payouts? Will the budget be prepared to favour the bonus plan or the business plan? Good questions.

It might be a sound idea to link bonuses to line-by-line achievement of budgeted items. The manager who has very little variance between the budgeted items and actual results demonstrates a sound understanding of the business environment.

12.7 Conclusion

In this chapter we have examined the basic budgeting model and emphasised the importance of honesty in setting out and achieving your plan to meet the objectives.

We touched on the typical pitfalls that cause budgeting to be such a protracted exercise and the fact that these delays result in the world having changed before the budgets are even completed.

Finally we discussed an alternative methodology that rewards managers for accurately achieving the detailed plan rather than rewarding them on overall profit only.

Whatever your particular scenario is, if the budgeting process is not yielding the results then it may be time to review its effectiveness.

Notes for my business plan

13 WRAP UP

We set out by stating that budgets should commence with the profit objectives and work back to calculating the contribution and revenue needed to cover the returns and any increases in expenses.

The concept is that profit + expenses = contribution from sales.

We then looked at how to calculate the additional sales required to cover extra expenses and maintain the operating profit or breakeven on profit. We just divide the extra expenses by the contribution percentage.

This will achieve the objective but we found that the ROS percentage decreased as the same profit amount is now expressed as a percentage of a higher revenue amount. This led us to the formula for calculating the extra revenue to cover the extra expense and maintain the ROS percentage. The extra expense is divided by the difference between the contribution percentage and the target profit percentage.

You then had a look at the implications of tax and how to adjust after tax returns to the before tax returns as shown in the NIBT. You learnt how to use the common size percentages to solve the extra sales if tax rates and/or contribution percentages changed.

Finally, you worked through the steps required to determine how much we must sell to satisfy shareholder expectations.

By using these formulas you will have a much better handle on the business and a deeper understanding of the connection between sale activities and company objectives.

In closing we introduced some tips on improving the budgeting process and adding some fun into the business process. Whilst business is not primarily about formulas and sums they do still provide the professional manager with the foundation for sound, well-considered, business decisions.

14 ANSWERS TO EXERCISES

Answers to Exercise 1   Understanding cost behaviour

	F	V	S	SV
Wages	X			
Quality control	X			
Warehouse costs			X	
Cost of sales		X		
Outsourced transport				X
Service desks			X	
Office space for growing sales force			X	
Depreciation	X			
Royalties on sales		X		
Consultants fees	X			

Answers to Exercise 2   Calculating sales revenue

Scenario 1:

You are selling products with an average gross profit percentage of 28%. The owners of the business require an operating profit of R1 500 000 per annum and you need to cover monthly running expenses of R200 000.

How much must you sell in total value?

Operating profit target	R1 500 000 +
Fixed costs R200 000 x 12	R2 400 000 +
Equals gross profit required	R3 900 000 =
Divided by gross profit %	28.0%÷
Equals total sales revenue	R13 928 571 =

Result

Remember if gross profit = 28% then cost of sales must be:

100% - 28% = 72%

Equals total sales revenue	R13 928 571
Cost of sales 72%	R10 028 571
Equals gross profit required	R3 900 000
Fixed costs R200 000 x 12	R2 400 000
Equals operating profit	R1 500 000

Scenario 2:

The average cost of sales for your products is 70%. The owners of the business require an operating profit of R1 500 000 per annum and you need to cover monthly running expenses of R200 000.

How much must you sell in total value?

Operating profit target	R1 500 000 +
Fixed costs R200 000 x 12	R2 400 000 +
Equals gross profit required	R3 900 000 =
Divided by gross profit %	30.0%÷
Equals total sales revenue	R13 000 000 =

Result

Remember if cost of sales is 70% then gross profit must be:

100% - 70% = 30%

Equals total sales revenue	R13 000 000
Cost of sales 70%	R9 100 000
Equals gross profit required	R3 900 000
Fixed costs R200 000 x 12	R2 400 000
Equals operating profit	R1 500 000

How did you go? This is a key concept so make sure you thoroughly understand the logic.

Using the data in the table, calculate the minimum number of units for the company to break even.

The selling price is the market average + 15% due to our added value = R295.00

Company A : Break Even Analysis	
SG & A costs	250 000,00
Unit cost price	178,23
Average market selling price	256,52
Added value over market average	15%
Calculate the selling price	295,00
Enter the unit cost price	-178,23
Calculate the unit gross profit	116,77
Enter SG & A costs	250 000,00
Divided by unit GP value	116,77
Equals the nNumber of units	**2141**

Answers to Exercise 4   Units to cover profit and costs

Using the data in the table, calculate the minimum number of units for the company to achieve the operating profit target. Remember to allow for the sales commission paid on each unit sold.

Remember that sales commission is a variable cost of selling price.

Company A : Units to meet OP target	
SG & A costs	250 000,00
Operating profit target	120 000,00
Unit cost price	178,23
Average market selling price	256,52
Sales commission	2%
Added value over market average	15%
Calculate the selling price	295,00
Enter the unit cost price	-178,23
Calculate the sales commission	-5,90
Calculate unit gross contribution	110,87
Enter the SG & A costs	250 000,00
Plus operating profit target	120 000,00
Equals gross profit target	370 000,00
Divided by unit contribution	110,87
Equals the number of units	3337

Answers to Exercise 5   Determine unit sales for multiple groups

Using the data in the table below calculate how many units each product group needs to sell:

	Group A	Group B	Group C	Group D
Average GP%	27,0%	32,0%	18,0%	22,0%
Average commission %	2,0%	2,5%	2,0%	2,0%
Contribution % of sales	25,0%	29,5%	16,0%	20,0%
Company operating profit	R 12 000 000,00			
Company SG & A costs	R 36 000 000,00			
Company Contribution	R 48 000 000,00			
	Group A	Group B	Group C	Group D
Portion of total contribution	15,0%	12,0%	28,0%	45,0%
Contribution amount	R 7 200 000	R 5 760 000	R 13 440 000	R 21 600 000
Divided by % contribution	25,0%	29,5%	16,0%	20,0%
Equals total sales of	R 28 800 000	R 19 525 424	R 84 000 000	R 108 000 000
Average selling price	R 175,00	R 210,00	R 238,00	R 410,00
Total average units	164 571	92 978	352 941	263 415

Step 1.   Calculate the contribution % for each group:
Average GP% - Average Commission % = Average Contribution % of sales.
27% - 2% = 25% contribution for Group A.

Step 2.   Add company operating profit and company SG & A costs
R12 000 000 + R36 000 000 = R48 000 000 total company contribution

Step 3 Apportion total company contribution to each group
R48 000 000 x 15% = R7 200 000 contribution from Group A

Step 4.   Divide group contribution by group contribution %
R7 200 000 ÷ 25% = R28 800 000 for Group A

Step 5.   Group sales revenue divided by average selling price equals average units for the group
R28 800 000 ÷ R175.00 = 164 571 units for Group A

Test the units against capacity and the market to validate the result as being achievable.

Answers to Exercise 6   DOL

	Company A	Company B
Sales revenue	285 000	465 000
Cost of sales	185 250	176 700
Gross profit	99 750	288 300
Sales commission	5 700	16 275
Contribution	94 050	272 025
Bank charges	1 560	4 500
Advertising	12 000	56 000
Auditors fees	5 632	5 632
Rent	5 000	5 000
Salaries and wages	15 000	106 000
Insurance	22 236	22 236
Operating profit	32 622	72 657
Interest expense	5 600	4 231
NIBT	27 022	68 426

	Question	Company A	Company B
1	Calculate the degree of operating leverage for the two companies.	94 050 ÷ 32 622 = 2.88	272 025 ÷ 72 657 = 3.74
2	Which company would benefit more from an increase in sales?	Company B due to higher DOL	
3	Sales increase by 12%. How much will each company's operating profit increase?	12 x 2.88 = 34.56%	12 x 3.74 = 44.8%
4	If Company B wants to increase operating profit by 10%, how much more must they sell percentage wise?	10 ÷ 3.74 = 2.67% more sales	

1. Total contribution = SG&A + operating profit

2. R400 000 + R 250 000 = R 650 000 contribution

3. Sales revenue = contribution ÷ contribution %

4. Scenario A: R650 000 ÷ 28% = R2 321 429.

5. Enter as Sales revenue under Proof.

6. Apply the common size percentages to sales revenue to complete the values in the "Proof" income statement

	Scenario 1		Scenario 2		Scenario 3	
Gross profit		30,00%		15,00%		25,00%
Commission		2,00%		0,00%		2,00%
Contribution		28,00%		15,00%		23,00%
SG & A expenses		400 000		400 000		400 000
Operating profit		250 000		250 000		250 000
Sales revenue required		2 321 429		4 333 333		2 826 087
	CS %	Proof	CS %	Proof	CS %	Proof
Sales revenue	100%	2 321 429	100%	4 333 333	100%	2 826 087
Cost of sales	70%	1 625 000	85%	3 683 333	75%	2 119 565
Gross profit	30%	696 429	15%	650 000	25%	706 522
Commission	2%	46 429	0%	-	2%	56 522
Calculated contribution	28%	650 000	15%	650 000	23%	650 000
Required contribution		650 000		650 000		650 000
SG & A expenses		400 000		400 000		400 000
Operating profit		250 000		250 000		250 000

Which business would you prefer? Hopefully you chose Scenario 1.

Answers to Exercise 8   Impact on working capital

Step 1.   Calculate the new sales figure for next year.

R4 571 190 + 15% = R5 256 869

Step 2.   Daily sales equals R5 256 869 ÷ 365 = R14 402

Daily Cost of Sales = R10 116

Step 3.   Accounts receivable will be:

R14 402.38 x 48 days = R691 314

Step 4.   Inventory days will be:

R10 116.41 x 73 days = R738 498

Step 5.   Accounts payable will be:

R10 116.41 x 45 days = R455 238

Step 6.   The additional working capital required next year will be:

R974 574 – R737 120 = R237 454

Income Statement	This Year		Next Year	
	Annual	Daily	Annual	Daily
Sales Revenue	R 4 571 190	R 12 524	R 5 256 869	R 14 402,38
Cost of sales	R 3 210 859	R 8 797	R 3 692 488	R 10 116,41
Balance sheet	Balance	Days	Balance	Days
Accounts receivable	R 526 000	42	R 691 314	48
Inventory	R 563 000	64	R 738 498	73
Current assets	R 1 089 000	106	R 1 429 812	121
Accounts payable	R 351 880	40	R 455 238	45
Current liabilities	R 351 880	40	R 455 238	45
Working capital	R 737 120	66,00	R 974 574	76,00

Working capital would increase by   R   237 454

Answers to Exercise 9   Effect of discounts

A. Discount 5% and contribution is 22.5% therefore increased sales value is:

$$5\% \div (22.5\% - 5\%) \text{ or } 5\% \div 17.5\% = 28.6\%$$

New sales revenue = R7 316 341

		Discount allowed>>>>		5,00%	
		C/S %	C/S %	Amounts	
Sales revenue	5 689 223	100%	100,00%	R 7 316 341	
Cost of sales	4 266 917	75,0%	80,00%	R 5 853 073	
Gross profit	1 422 306	25,0%	20,00%	R 1 463 268	
Commission	142 231	2,5%	2,50%	R 182 909	
Contribution	1 280 075	22,5%	17,50%	R 1 280 360	
SG & A expenses	853 210	15,0%	11,66%	R 853 210	
Operating profit	426 865	7,5%	5,83%	R 426 865	

B. Discount 7.5% and contribution is 22.5% therefore increased sales value is:

$$7.5\% \div (22.5\% - 7.5\%) \text{ or } 7.5\% \div 15\% = 50\%$$

New sales revenue = R8 533 835

		Discount allowed>>>>		7,50%	
		C/S %	C/S %	Amounts	
Sales revenue	5 689 223	100%	100,00%	R 8 533 835	
Cost of sales	4 266 917	75,0%	82,50%	R 7 040 413	
Gross profit	1 422 306	25,0%	17,50%	R 1 493 421	
Commission	142 231	2,5%	2,50%	R 213 346	
Contribution	1 280 075	22,5%	15,00%	R 1 280 075	
SG & A expenses	853 210	15,0%	10,00%	R 853 210	
Operating profit	426 865	7,5%	5,00%	R 426 865	

Answers to Exercise 10   Effect of discounts on ROWC

Using the data in the table below calculate the working capital value before the discount is allowed. For the exercise you use 300 trading days to calculate the daily sales and daily cost of sales. Complete the exercise after the 7.5% discount is allowed and then complete the answers below:

Discount	Before Discount		After Discount	
7.50%	Amount	CS%	Amount	CS%
Sales revenue	R 570 000.00	100.0%	R 760 000.00	100.0%
Cost of sales	R 399 000.00	70.0%	R 589 000.00	77.5%
Gross profit	R 171 000.00	30.0%	R 171 000.00	22.5%
SG&A	R 38 000.00	6.7%	R 38 000.00	5.0%
Operating profit	R 133 000.00	23.3%	R 133 000.00	17.5%
Balance Sheet Data		days		days
Accounts receivable	R 95 000.00	50.00	R 126 666.67	50.00
Inventory	R 99 750.00	75.00	R 147 250.00	75.00
Current assets	R 194 750.00	125.00	R 273 916.67	
Accounts payable	R 79 800.00	60.00	R 117 800.00	60.00
Current liabilities	R 79 800.00	60.00	R 117 800.00	
Working capital	R 114 950.00	65.00	R 156 116.67	65.00
ROWC	115.70%		85.19%	
WC % of sales	20.17%		20.54%	

1	What is the new percentage operating profit ROS?	17.5%
2	How much more must we sell to make the same operating profit?	R190 000
3	How much cash did the change in working capital require?	R41 116.67
4	Calculate the ROWC after the discount.	85.19%
5	Did the WC% of sales change significantly?	No

Answers to Exercise 11   Expenses change – how must we sell to break even

Part a - Salaries are expected to increase by 8% next year and wages by 8.5%.

1. Income statement should contain this data. The Original is before the increased staff costs.

	Original		CS %	Revised		CS %
Revenue	R	385 000	100,00%	R	401 141	100,00%
COS	R	261 800	68,00%	R	272 776	68,00%
Gross profit	**R**	**123 200**	**32,00%**	**R**	**128 365**	32,00%
Commission	R	7 700	2,00%	R	8 023	2,00%
Contribution	**R**	**115 500**	**30,00%**	**R**	**120 342**	30,00%
Advertising	R	2 865	0,74%	R	2 865	0,71%
Bank charges	R	1 389	0,36%	R	1 389	0,35%
Rent	R	5 500	1,43%	R	5 500	1,37%
Wages	R	32 000	8,31%	R	34 720	8,66%
Depreciation	R	6 500	1,69%	R	6 500	1,62%
Salaries	R	26 530	6,89%	R	28 652	7,14%
Operating profit	**R**	**40 716**	**10,58%**	**R**	**40 716**	10,15%
Interest expense	R	1 668	0,43%	R	1 668	0,42%
Other income	R	4 000	1,04%	R	4 000	1,00%
NIBT	**R**	**43 048**	**11,18%**	**R**	**43 048**	10,73%
Tax	R	12 914	3,35%	R	12 914	3,22%
Net income	**R**	**30 134**	**7,83%**	**R**	**30 134**	7,51%

2. At current GP% margins the increased staff expenses of R4 842 would require:

R4 842 ÷ 30% contribution = R16 140 extra sales.

3. If margins dropped to 30% then the extra sales on R385 000 would be:

R4 842 ÷ 28% contribution = R17 293

Answers to Exercise 12   Expenses change – how much must we sell to maintain ROS%

Step 1. Calculate the TECS% between Contribution and NIBT

30% - 12% = 18.00% at bottom of spreadsheet.

Step 2: Calculate the changes to costs and other income:

SG&A costs + interest expense – other income

R4 822 + R0 – R800 = R4 042 in cell column "Change" and row "NIBT"

Step 3: Total net costs ÷ TECS% = Additional revenue

R4 042 ÷ 18.0% = R22 458 additional revenue

	Original	CS %	Change	Revised	CS %
Revenue	R 385 000	100,00%	R 22 458	R 407 458	100,00%
COS	R 261 800	68,00%	R 15 271	R 277 071	68,00%
Gross profit	R 123 200	32,00%	R 7 186	R 130 386	32,00%
Commission	R 7 700	2,00%	R 449	R 8 149	2,00%
Contribution	R 115 500	30,00%	R 6 737	R 122 237	30,00%
Advertising	R 2 865	0,74%	R -	R 2 865	0,70%
Bank charges	R 1 389	0,36%	R -	R 1 389	0,34%
Rent	R 3 866	1,00%	R -	R 3 866	0,95%
Wages	R 32 000	8,31%	R 2 720	R 34 720	8,52%
Depreciation	R 6 500	1,69%	R -	R 6 500	1,60%
Salaries	R 26 530	6,89%	R 2 122	R 28 652	7,03%
Operating profit	R 42 350	11,00%	R 4 842	R 44 245	10,86%
Interest expense	R -1 668	-0,43%	R -	R -1 668	-0,41%
Other Income	R 5 518	1,43%	R -800	R 6 318	1,55%
NIBT	R 46 200	12,00%	R 4 042	R 48 895	12,00%
Tax	R 13 860	3,60%	R 1 213	R 14 668	3,60%
Net income	R 32 340	8,40%	R 2 830	R 34 226	8,40%
TCCS% from Contribution to NIBT			18,00%	Mission accomplished	

Answers to Exercise 13 Meeting shareholders' expectations

How much must they sell to meet shareholder expectations?

Step 1. Earnings per share are calculated as being:

number of share x planned EPS

10 000 000 x 24 cents(20% more than prior 20cents per share)

=R2 400 000 net income.

Step 2   ROI is required to be 10%. Inflation rate of 8% x 1.25.

Total investment is R9 000 000 + R6 000 000 + R8 000 000

=R23 000 000 x 10% = R2 3000 000 net income

Step 3   We will use ROI of R2 400 000 as the net income target as it is higher than the EPS target and so will satisfy both criteria.

We can now apply the logic in the spreadsheet on the next page.

Step		Data	Values	CS%
1	Net income after tax	71,0%	R 2 400 000	3,33%
	Tax rate	29,0%	R 980 282	1,36%
2	Net income before tax	100,0%	R 3 380 282	4,68%
	Interest expense		R 600 000	0,83%
3	Operating profit		R 3 980 282	5,51%
	SG&A expenses		R 8 650 000	11,99%
4	Contribution	17,5%	R 12 630 282	17,50%
7	Commission	2,5%	R 1 804 326	2,50%
	Gross profit	20,0%	R 14 434 608	20,00%
6	Cost of sales	80,0%	R 57 738 431	80,00%
5	**Sales revenue**	**100,0%**	**R 72 173 038**	100,00%

Step 1. Enter net income

Step 2. Calculate NIBT (NI ÷ 71%)

Step 3. Add interest expense to NIBT = operating profit

Step 4. Add SG&A expenses to operating profit = contribution

Step 5.   Contribution ÷ contribution % = sales revenue

Step 6.   Sales revenue x COS % = cost of sales value

Step 7.   Sales revenue – COS = gross profit

Step 8   Sales revenue x commission % = commission

Step 9.   Gross profit – commission = contribution

ABOUT THE AUTHOR

Ronnie was involved in the IT industry for over 20 years starting as a sales trainee with an international IT company and moving up the ranks through sales manager, national sales manager to strategic marketing manager over a period of about eight years.

He attended the Graduate School of Business PMD course at the University of Cape Town. In 1982 he received the merit award for Marketing from the IMM and wrote a paper on "Consumer vs Industrial Marketing" which was nominated for the Raymond Ackerman marketing award.

Ronnie expanded his knowledge of production and manufacturing by qualifying as a member of the American Production & Inventory Control Society [CPIM] in 1989.

He started Business Learning Systems Sa cc in 1990 specialising in Business and Sales Training.

After training the scientists and engineers at the Atomic Energy Corporation in business practices he was appointed as the consulting Sales Manager at the AEC for the 11 divisions that were entering the commercial market.

In 1995 he was appointed managing director of a medium sized engineering company where he was able to successfully implement and test the concepts he taught on his business courses.

Within two years the company reduced manufacturing lead times from 16 weeks to three weeks and improved on-time deliveries from being an average of two to three weeks late to 78% being delivered on due day. Sales were also improved by 35% over the period.

In July 2010 Ronnie successfully completed the CSCP exam certifying him as Supply Chain Professional to add to his CPIM qualification. He later became a Demand Driven Professional by acquiring his CDDP certification.

He also works with Brian Maskell and Associates presenting their workshops on Lean Management and Value Stream Costing for lean manufacturing operations and is their appointed consultant in South Africa.

More recently he has also been qualified through the International Purchasing and Supply Chain Management Institute as a Certified International Supply Chain Professional.

With qualifications and practical experience in manufacturing, supply chain management, marketing and sales from sales trainee to managing director, Ronnie brings a wealth of practical experience to his training programmes in finance, supply chain and production.

Ronnie Davidson

(IMM, CPIM, CSCP , CDDP, CISCM & CISCP)